No Second Chance

Antrina L. Harris

DMJ Publishing & Web Design

Printed in the United States of America

First Printing, 2017 (written in 1996)

DMJ Publishing & Web Design
wwwdmjpublishing.com

Available from Amazon.com and other retail outlets

Cover Design by:
Robert C. Jacobs
rob397@gmail.com

This book is dedicated to God my Father, who is also God the Father God, God the Son who is also my elder brother and God the Holy Spirit who is my best friend. Without you I would not have taken the stand to start this book or had the nerve to complete it. Thank you for standing with me.

ACKNOWLEDGEMENTS

I want to acknowledge my husband, Charles, for his encouragement to me to complete the book.

My son, Damon, who jumped on the bandwagon of encouragement and continued to say, "You can do it, mom and this book is finished."

Chuck III (my grandson), thank you for being my typist and my teacher on the computer.

Chuck, Jr. thanks for standing for me in the spiritual realm watching my back at all times.

Contents

Never Ending Chapter *9*

Never Ending Chapter

It is a cool, crisp autumn morning. The sun has not risen. It is still early morning. You can smell the cool, fresh air; feel the moisture on your skin.

For some reason, it was very quiet outside. There was no traffic, not even birds chirping. It seemed to be a very strange morning like there was something hovering in the air. You couldn't quite make it out but it seemed to be directed toward this one house in particular. The mist around this house was different than the rest of the moisture in the air. It was thick and gray. It almost looked like fog; but it wasn't fog. It looked like smoke from a smothered fire; but it didn't smell like smoke. It had the smell of flowers in a funeral home. It made your skin seemingly crawl. The smell also had an odor of something that was either dying or had just died.

The house was completely dark, except for the dimly lit back bedroom on the second floor. In the room was a young woman sitting in the middle of the bed with her legs crossed beneath her. She was very frail. Her face looked haggard and tired. She wanted to cry but she was too depressed to even try. The young lady, at one time, was very pretty. She is also highly educated. She is ready to enter a graduate school of law but there is a problem.

There is something in her hand. At a closer glance, you can see it is a crack vial. She seemed to be hesitating about popping the vial. She was getting more depressed by the second. Slowly, she reached for the pipe but quickly drew her hand away. She tried talking to herself, "Lisa, you can make it. Be strong. Why didn't you stay in the rehab program? You only had three months to go. Why did you leave? Now you are being tempted and you are getting weak. Lisa, don't give in to crack." She was scared.

Lisa remembered a voice in the back of her mind. It seemed to be a deadly warning to her. She sat up straight, trying to remember the warning. The strange voice said, "If you do drugs again, you will die and go to hell where you will spend forever with your eternal father." Her insides shuddered with this awful thought. Then she shrugged and thought to herself, "There is only one me."

In the meantime, the unusual mist was becoming very dense around Lisa's house. Standing beside the oak tree in Lisa's backyard was a tall figure. At first, it just looked like a man was peering up toward her bedroom window. Your first thought would be there's a Peeping Tom; someone should call the police. But when you look closer you realize it is not a man. It is the Spirit of Death. It is at least six feet tall, dressed in a shade of black that cannot be described by natural colors. The black seems to be covered in a coldness that is not of this world.

At first, you think the flesh is just pale; however, there is no flesh. It is almost like a shadow with a smile on a face so hideous that it would make the bravest man scream. The spirit of death is waiting; just standing there waiting for its next victim. You can hear a chuckle coming from its throat as it waits in anticipation. The chuckle turns into a loud, roaring laugh. Death thinks to itself, "I have her now. There is no turning back. She is weak and ready to break."

Death looks over its shoulder. Behind him, standing in the shadow of a tall shrub plant, is another figure. Death states, "You have done it again. Good for you. She's as good as dead. You do your part and I'll go collect her." The figure comes out of the shadows dressed in clothing that could be made from the earth's finest material and wearing a gold chain. There were gold rings on both hands. There was also another ring on its hand with a large ruby that was very hypnotic. Even so, he was overdressed, cheap-looking and wearing too much jewelry. As a matter of fact, he reminded you of a pimp or hustler. With a smug look and smile on his face, he simply said, "I know. It is just a matter of time now, just a matter of time."

Inside, Lisa felt a peculiar chill go through her body. She thinks within herself, "I am too young to die. I am only 20 years old. I have never been married and I do not even have a child to call me mom. I can't die. If you hear me, God, Help Me Please!"

Outside, this got the attention of Death and the Spirit of Drugs; better known as "Kingpin." They did not like the sound of that. Death became agitated and angry. He began yelling at Kingpin, "You are losing her. Do something!" Kingpin yells thoughts into Lisa's room, "You have a hit of White China in your dresser drawer. Get it! This is not the same as crack. You know this is a better rush and the voices didn't tell you that China White would kill you." Death smiles and tells Kingpin, "Nice job."

Lisa came to the conclusion that her mother doesn't know anything and that her prayers are worthless. She thinks, "The church didn't do me any good. Where is God (if there is a God)?" Death and Kingpin laugh and think, "Good for you. Good for you. That's the right thought, 'there is no God'. What has He done for you?"

Lisa thinks this is her thought, "Yes, what has He done for me, if He exists? Oh well, I won't chance Crack just in case there is death in it; but I do have something new in my dresser that I haven't tried yet. I hear it is a great rush. Ok Lisa, go for it! What harm can it do? I hear the rush is better than crack."

The event happened so quickly. Like a flash, she is off her bed and across the room. She opens her drawer and takes out the China White. Back on her bed, she prepares the China White for her use.

She ties off her vein with a rubber hose and inserts the needle. Lisa screams "Oh no, something is wrong!" There is a pause. Death states, "That is my cue." It seems that her dealer always greeted her with those same words and with that same smile. Kingpin realized she recognized those words. And, of course, he and Death laugh again. They were having great fun at her expense. Do not be fooled by all of this laughter. They are not friends but natural enemies. At this point, they are working together because Lisa is a great prize for their master. Lisa's mother was a prayer warrior. They hated her with a passion. To win Lisa for their master was a great reward for them. If they had not won Lisa, she would have been a great thorn in their side.

Death says to Kingpin, "Here is the prize our Master has been waiting for." Kingpin hisses "Yessss, here is the prize. Come, Lisa, the Master awaits." She pulls back screaming all the more and louder but to no avail. She is pulled into the opening in the earth. She thinks, "This is my backyard. How can this be?" Kingpin just says, "If you had accepted my natural enemy as your savior, you would head up; but you didn't. So now you head down. Whichever Master you choose determines the direction. You see, Lisa, this is no longer your backyard, but the entrance to Hell!"

Lisa felt herself falling, falling falling. She thought, "When will I land and stop this descent? It seems to go on forever." The further down she went, the darker it became. She also noticed it was becoming hotter. Lisa thought that, according to earth's time, they had been descending for about 8 hours. Lisa turned her head as if she was listening for something. She noticed they were slowing down and it was so hot. She still had on, she thought, the mini skirt and sweater she was wearing when she died. Lisa thought, "I'm glad I am barefooted. It is so hot. Why did I choose Hell? Why?"

Approximately 12 earth hours had passed when, suddenly, they stopped. Kingpin continued to hold onto Lisa's hand. Lisa again tried to pull away, but his grip tightened. Her shrieking was disheartening. "God help me, please help me; I'm so sorry. Please forgive me, I didn't know. How could I know that this is real? People kept saying Hell is on earth. They kept saying there is no life after death. They kept saying we could be reincarnated. They said we are our own God; one with the universe. I didn't know. Help me, please!" Lisa did not receive an answer, only the tug on her arm.

* * * * *

Lisa found herself in front of the entrance to Hell. She was taken inside. Kingpin looked at her and remarked in a cold voice, "There is someone who is anticipating your arrival. Come meet your Master." As she looked around, Lisa noticed what seemed to be different levels; some more torturous than others. She realized she still had not seen all of Hell. They came to a very large entrance. Inside, sitting on a very high throne, was a surprisingly handsome being. She thought, "If this is Satan, he looks nothing like the pictures I've seen of him."

Satan looked down at Lisa and said, very subtly, "Welcome home my dear child." Almost in shock, Lisa looked around. Satan didn't have a pitch fork, he didn't have a tail and pointed ears. He was a beautiful angel with lovely wings. He was hypnotic in appearance. But she took notice of his eyes. They were full of evil and hate. The closer she was pulled to him by an invisible force, the more she felt there was such an evil about him. As Lisa looked around, she noticed furniture – a long table with chairs around it. What looked like different kinds of jewels were scattered around the room. Satan was robed like a king; nothing like Kingpin, who looked cheap by comparison.

Satan lets Kingpin know he is pleased with him. He tells Kingpin he will sit in chair 2 at the conference table instead of chair 3. Satan told Kingpin that if he keeps up the good work he will be in the 1st chair. But to do that, he must get more children of those meddling, praying, wailing Christians. He told Kingpin, "They are my worst enemies. They just pray and talk to my number one enemy all the time. And what gets on my nerves is, He answers them! I hate Bible-reading, praying Christians."

Kingpin responded, "When some Christians pray and read the bible it doesn't seem to bother you." Satan said, "True, but that's because they do not pray in power and strength. They just say words and read words. They do not understand who God is. I am talking about those who know what they have in that Book and know how to get God's attention in prayer. Kingpin, I want you to go and launch an all-out assault on them. Do you want Chair 1? If you want first place at the table, go get them."

Kingpin leaves the throne room and heads for earth once more. His plan is to assault another member of Lisa's family, but this time in a more gruesome, heartless way.

There are some helpers waiting for him.

* * * * *

It is now 5:00 a.m. in the town called Halal-Land. Haw-lal means Praise. In essence, the town is really named Praise-Land.

Halal-Land is a fairly large city. It is a place for people with expensive tastes. The city is for those who like a faster pace. The outskirts of the city are for those who like city dwelling but also desire the quiet life. There are suburbs for those who prefer living away from city. Then there are rural areas for those who like quiet, fresh air and country living. Halal-Land has many choices to satisfy different tastes. It is a very prosperous city. Many businesses and banks were established in Halal-Land. If you just judged by the scene in the natural realm and not by the unseen realm, everything seemed fine in Halal-Land.

There were many churches of all denominations in this city but something was extremely wrong. For the most part, the churches had become what the Bible refers to as lukewarm. There were many churchgoers but not many Christians.

One church was on 43rd Street & Cherry Tree Lane. It was ordinary looking and didn't have an overly large congregation. The pastor of this church, Jerry Green, believed in prayer and Bible study in his private time and also for his congregation. He spent lots of time on his face before God. He knew something was going on in Halal-Land and it disturbed him. But he did not quite know what it was.

On this particular day, November 5th, the pastor was just sitting in the church wondering what had happened. He knew something awful had taken place. There was a smell in the air. He thought it smelled like something he had smelled before but there was another odor with it. He looked at his watch. It was 5:45 am.

Suddenly Lisa's mother, Karen Kingslei, awakens with a start. She is scared and cannot figure out the reason for it. She is crying uncontrollably. She sits up in the bed and hangs her feet over the side. For some reason she does not want to move. Softly, she calls Lisa. Somewhat louder, she calls again and asks what she wants for breakfast. Lisa did not answer. Mrs. Kingslei slowly gets out of her bed and stands by the side of the bed. Her legs feel heavy like weights. She thinks to herself, "Alright Karen, get yourself together."

She hesitated then headed down the hall to Lisa's bedroom. She knew in her heart of hearts something was desperately wrong. She was almost in front of Lisa's door and noticed it was slightly cracked open. Mrs. Kingslei took a deep breath and knocked softly on the door. Lisa didn't answer but the door pushed open under the firmness of her knock.

Mrs. Kingslei's eyes became fixed on Lisa's bed. She could not believe what she saw. Her words came ever so softly from her mouth, "Oh Lisa baby, how could you do this to yourself? God, Father, Jesus, Lord is she really dead?" Karen Kingslei knew the answer to her question, even before she moved over to her only daughter's bed and saw her lifeless body. To Lisa's mother, the bed appeared to be an open grave. Tears rolled down her face as she reached out and touched the cold, lifeless body of her baby. She thinks to herself "Oh God, she must have been dead for a while." Just like a loving mother, Mrs. Kingslei reaches out and gathers a blanket to cover the body.

Karen sits on the bed next to Lisa's body. She takes hold of her baby's hand and softly weeps. "Oh God, why?" As Karen sits there a thought comes to her, "Is this my fault in some way?" She begins to reflect on her life and everything she used to associate with herself. Sex and shopping were the most important things in her life when she was Lisa's age. It did not matter who she was having sex with. Sex was just sex in her old life. "Is this really my fault? Is this what Lisa was rebelling against?" She truly did not know.

By the time Karen realized that her baby was in trouble, it was too late. Lisa did not care about education because it came easy to her. All she wanted was drugs, drugs, and more drugs. Karen remembered her promise to God. Her question to God was, "How will I fulfill this promise?" In her mind, she was stuck on the thought that, because of her past lifestyle, this must in some way be her fault. She'd thought that if she kept quiet it would just go away. She resolves within herself, "I will do whatever I have to do to help other young adults. Now I know what I must strive to do and I am ready to take the steps to do it, for my Lisa and all the other Lisas in the world."

Then she reached for the phone and dialed 911. Her voice trails off as she reports the death of her daughter.

* * * * *

As this scene is taking place on earth, Lisa is watching in stark disbelief. But she has to believe, for she is watching it take place from the portal of hell.

"Miss Kingslei, I presume," Satan says in a sarcastic manner as Lisa looks up. She noticed he was no longer seated, but was standing in front of her. "Well, Miss Kingslei, are you ready to go into your living quarters? Of course you realize you do not have a choice in the matter. Let's go. I want to escort you personally. I thought, at one point, I was going to lose you. Do you remember ALL of your mother's prayers? There was a moment back in August you almost gave your life to my enemy; but I won. You see, I am the king, not Jesus. Well at least, I am your king. Bow your knees to me. You no good #$@&%*! He uses words that cannot be uttered in earthly words. Lisa was forced to bow her knee and worship him. He grabbed her by the scruff of her neck to lead her to her compartment of torment.

Lisa is very quiet, sobbing softly within herself. She realizes there is no more hope for her. As they walked deeper into the pit of Hell, it became hotter and darker.

When Satan reached the part of Hell that was to be home for Lisa, he stopped and looked at her for what seemed to be a very long moment. Then he lifted his foot and kicked her into a deep hole. When she landed, she looked around. There were personal demons assigned to torment her. There were only two of them but they were so large they took up much of her space. Whenever they wanted, they took up all of the compartment and just enveloped her.

Both spirits were about the same size in height. They stood at least ten feet tall. Their shapes reminded her of football players. One looked like a quarterback and the other like a linebacker.

The spirt that resembled a quarterback was of course the dominant spirit. The other was in the same rank of those called power spirits. Power was dressed in a brown so dreary that no color on earth could readily be compared to it. His face had the same appearance or structure as a human being. His dark, cold eyes displayed no feelings. He was as evil as evil could be. If you looked closely, you could see worms crawling out of his eye sockets, ears and the top of his head. He had an odor that reminded one of a filthy garbage can on a hot summer day, maggots and all.

The dominant spirit was dressed in a black color that could only come from hell itself. Even the Spirit of Death's black could not be compared to this color. There are no words that adequately describe it. His fingernails were very long and sharp. They resembled eagle claws and he knew how to expertly use them.

When he spoke, icicles formed around his words. The odor emanating from his person was sickeningly sweet. The overwhelmingly sweet odor from the spirit on her right was in complete contrast to the foul odor of the spirit on her left.

These two spirits could do whatever they wanted to do to Lisa for all eternity. They stood by Lisa – one on her right, the other on her left. They were looking down on her, scoffing and sneering. The dominant spirit was called Prince of the Night. He reminded Lisa how much she loved the night life. He told her it was his doing. Now she would be with him forever. Prince of the Night took his eagle-like claws and ripped at her face. He then ripped her from one end of her body to the other, causing her excruciating pain. Her moans emanated from deep within her very being.

Even her longing for drugs did not compare to this kind of pain. She cried out "There is pain in the belly of Hell. Why didn't I listen to my mother? Instead, I mocked her and her prayer partners. Oh God, help me!!" All of sudden, she felt a huge fist come across her face. It sent her tumbling over to the other side of her place of torment. When she hit the wall, hot coals and lava ran down her face and then slowly down the rest of her body.

She heard a voice say "Don't ever call on God. You are here in my domain. He has nothing to do with Hell." Lisa looked up into the face of Prince of the Night. Then she looked past him to see the other spirit. She wondered what it was doing. It looked as if he was scratching his head; but he had something in his hands. It was worms and they were alive. He held them over Lisa's head and let them fall on her. She jumped up and tried to get away. There was no getting away. As they attached themselves to her, it added to her torture.

* * * * *

Meanwhile, back on earth, Mrs. Kingslei waits for the coroner to come pick up Lisa's body. She is praying softly to herself. She is not questioning God because she knows God is the giver of life. Satan is the thief. Mrs. Kingslei knows it is Satan who has stolen her daughter from her. She makes this vow within herself; "He took my baby but I will reach into his kingdom and win every unbeliever I can, especially those who are lost to the drug world and to all the bondage which accompanies that way of life."

Mrs. Kingslei moves away from the window and slowly goes to her phone. She is getting ready to call her pastor. She knows he will be in his private prayer room in the sanctuary or in his office. If he is in the prayer room, he can still hear the phone. "Please God, let him answer; assure him it is an important call."

Karen Kingslei looked at her watch; it is 6:10 a.m. She thinks to herself, "He is still there. Lord, let him answer the phone." After dialing the office number, the phone rings one and a half times. Pastor Green picked up the phone. He hears Karen's voice, "Pastor Green, this is Karen Kingslei. Could you and Mrs. Green possibly come over to my house? Lisa has taken an overdose and she is dead." He told her they would be there within half an hour. After calling his wife, Leali, and informing her about the death of Lisa, he hung up the phone. All of a sudden it hit him; this is what had been disturbing him! He had picked up on Lisa's death in his spirit. He also realized what those two odors were. One was the odor of death and the other was the spirit of drugs.

Pastor Green picked up his wife and headed for Mrs. Kingslei's home. It was a very short drive although it seemed longer than it really was. They lived only a few blocks from each other. That particular area was known as "Churchgoers Row". Most people commented about the different feelings they experienced in that area. They claimed the air seemed cleaner and lighter. The spirit of the area was called "Holy". Some often referred to it as a place of refuge.

As they pulled into Karen Kingslei's driveway, Pastor Green spoke softly to his wife, "Let's go inside." They exited the car, stepped onto the porch and rang the doorbell. As they stood there in silent prayer, Karen opened the door. She fell into Leali's arms and cried. It felt as though her heart would burst open from the pain. Jerry and Leali cried with her.

Pastor Jerry Green looked down and observed Lisa's cold, dead body. She is no longer there. Lisa is truly dead to this world but alive in the spirit realm. She can hear them but they cannot hear her. Pastor Green slowly closes his eyes. It is difficult to look down at what used to be a vibrant healthy young life.

As he thinks this to himself, he suddenly is seeing himself as a youth in his college days… playing games, drinking, heavy drug use, living it up. If it was available, new or old, he had chosen to indulge in it. Whether he lived or died was completely up to him. At the time, it was about having fun. But was it real fun or an illusion? As Pastor Green continued thinking, he remembered how he almost partied himself right out of college. He remembered lying to his parents. He told them he was doing well in every class but he couldn't even remember what day of the week it was. When he was not indulging in his overuse of drugs, he was usually sleeping. Back then, in his mind, that was a happy lifestyle. These thoughts brought tears into the eyes of the distraught pastor as he whispered the most truthful words he'd spoken in a long time, "This could have been me."

Pastor Green remembered his parents confronting him about his dishonesty to them. At that point in his life, he couldn't have cared less what his parents had to say to him about their "Jesus" or, as they would say, Yeshua. He told his parents they could go to hell along with their Yeshua and, with that, his parents allowed God to deal with him directly. They removed their prayer covering over the young man and turned him over to his own desires. His parents told him to be careful of what he did and with whom he did it.

One evening, while at a party, he started to slip away. He did not realize he was indeed dying. He remembered hearing voices beckoning to him. They were telling him it was time to come home. Suddenly, as if shaking off a dream, he recognized who it was. He had heard these voices before. In no time at all, his pride had quickly turned to fear. He began to call out his parents' names and even Yeshua's name to ask for help. He was prepared to give his life fully over to the Lord at this point. He promised God that, if he spared his life, he would live the rest of it only for the one true Savior. As Green finished his promise of new life, he awoke with tears running wild on his face and cheeks flushed with red.

In this present moment, he realizes there is much to be done in this world. "What to do...how to do it?", he ponders silently. We need a lot of help. These youth are much wiser then we are. They seek truthful answers; not just the same crap that gets spoon fed to them every Sunday, the real truth. They understand the spirit world.

"Why Lisa?", Leali Green wonders with great sadness in her heart. "What has she done to deserve such a fate?" Leali would not sit down. She stood and just looked at what was once a beautiful young lady. Leali thinks back on her life when she was Lisa's age. She recalls never doing much of anything. Her parents were so religious and hardcore that they scared the hellfire out of her. She never had much fun or freedom. She just prayed very religious prayers and constantly went to church. She admits to herself, "I never really knew Jesus. I don't even know if I really know him right now, the way I really should. Yes I know and understand religion, but do I know him?

It's something to truly think about. I know Jerry has cheated because of my coldness. Thank God I am better. There is a lot to do. Am I up to the task? I believe I am. It is more than just going to church on Sunday and Monday. If we don't get this right, we are going to lose a generation of people. There is a strategy but I haven't learned it yet. One day, I will learn and perfect it. For every young life lost, one life will be gained. God will show me not how to lose, but how to win. This is not my fight but Yeshua's fight. God, help me to be strong and brave for you. I will fight for you and even die if you deem it so."

Finally, they made their way into the front room. Karen and Leali sat on the couch and Jerry sat on a lounge chair next to them. Karen described to them what happened down to the smallest detail. She told them about the feeling she had the day before and about the two odors she kept smelling. Pastor Green interrupted her at that point. He asked her about the feelings and the odors she smelled. When she described them, it was the same feeling he'd had and the exact same odors. He said softly, "There is a war going on in the spirit realm and we are experiencing it here on this earth. Satan is after our children and we'd better do battle as never before." He looked at his wife and Karen then said "It is either victory for us or defeat." Then he emphasized, "I mean all Christians, everywhere."

Before leaving, Pastor Green and Leali prayed for Karen. They asked God to strengthen her in her spirit, soul and body. They prayed especially for her soul. They asked God to give her the right scriptures to keep her emotions and thoughts intact. They prayed that she would battle in her prayer closet as never before. Pastor Green told Karen that as she went through the grieving stages, they would be there for her.

Within two days, Karen Kingslei had Lisa's funeral and burial. She did not want a long delay as it would be too painful. Her heart was aching. She felt as though her insides would explode. Karen had a private funeral and burial. She did not want any spectators.

After the funeral and burial, Leali went home with Karen. Her plan was to spend several days with her. She would spend a lot of time in intercession and warfare for Karen and for what was happening in their area. While in prayer, she began praying for Maria.

Maria, Karen's niece, is living with her. Maria's mother, who was Karen's sister, had died in a car accident.

* * * * *

In hell, Lisa walked over to a corner of her enclosure. There she sat on the floor and pulled her knees close to her chest.

She wrapped her arms tightly around her knees and placed her head down upon them. She started to sob within herself as she asked, "Why?"

All of a sudden Lisa stood up; her face mirrored disbelief. She was looking towards earth. She saw someone that she had thought did not exist. She started yelling, "Wait! Wait! I have to talk to you." Lisa did not get any response. She became angry and yelled even louder. "I said wait! I must speak to you!" He never even looked at Lisa. He kept his focus upon the earth. His eyes were roaming to and fro throughout the entire earth. Lisa stood still and said in a solemn voice, "The Holy Spirit is real. He is not a ghost but a person in this realm of the spirit. People fail to believe on the earth because they can't see Him; so they choose to disbelieve in His existence."

As Lisa looked toward Earth, she saw something quite disturbing…Christians who did not take winning the people with no hope seriously. They are too busy fighting amongst themselves and trying to believe for cars and furs. Trying to be head honchos with their pastors. Lisa thought to herself, "If Christians don't get their lives in order, there will be more Lisas in hell than I care to think about."

She did see some who were serious about winning the lost and hopeless. They were few in number. She chuckled at the thought that those who didn't care (and were doing the very things a lot of so-called sinners were doing) would be taking the express route to Hell. Then she laughed aloud at the thought. She stopped in disbelief when she realized that kind of laughter was coming from her. It reminded her of the Laughter of Hell and it was.

Lisa caught a glimpse of the Holy Spirit again. He kept His attention upon the earth. He acted as though He didn't even hear her. He totally ignored her. Lisa tried to hold a conversation with the Holy Spirit. She asked questions. She paused for a second, hoping He would say something, anything. He never did. She became incensed. What is wrong with you? I need answers. To the Holy Spirit, her questions were irrelevant.

Satan entered Lisa's room. He was very smug. He stood with his shoulders erect and head held high, with a half-smile on his face. As He waited, Lisa knew she had to bow and give him homage. She knew not to get up until He gave the word. Finally, in an insidious voice, he told her to rise.

Why are you trying to contact the Holy Spirit? I can answer any questions you may have for Him. First of all, let me show you a scene when you were in your mother's womb. Take a close look. A scene appeared out of nowhere. Lisa saw what seemed to be a baby happily playing in a woman's womb. Satan told her to take a closer look. As she looked closer, she realized it was her. She was so happy and content. It was so warm. She had just finished eating so she was full and, after playing, it was time for a nap.

Lisa realized her parents had wanted her and were eagerly awaiting her arrival. It was getting close to her birthing day. Inside she felt joy. She would look her mother in the face and nurse at her breast.

Her birth was very easy, not one complication. There was not one birthing problem. She was an average sized baby. Her lungs were very strong. So why did she turn out the way she did?

Satan looked at her and asked "Do you

want to see more?" She answered very humbly, "Yes, if it isn't any trouble." Lisa didn't want to upset her king. He stood there scrutinizing her for a moment, then proceeded to show her more of her past.

Lisa looked and saw herself as a toddler. Again, she saw how happy she was, playing at her mother's feet. Being cuddled by her mother. Snuggled in her mother's arms, asleep. She loved feeling the strong arms around her. It made her feel so secure. Lisa saw how much her mother and father played together, how they laughed together and how they prayed together. She realized when she was in the drug scene she had forgotten about the love of her parents. It all came back to her so painfully clear.

Then Satan spoke up and said, "That is enough for now." She bowed and kissed his hand. He told her to get up and follow him. With this command, she immediately got up and followed behind him. He strutted like a proud peacock and she walked very softly with her head hung down.

Satan entered his throne room then turned and looked at Lisa. He told her to sit down. She went to sit on one of the chairs and the next thing she remembered was lying face down on the floor with excruciating pain in her head and back. She heard her master's voice, "I didn't tell you to sit on a chair. You do not deserve a chair."

Then he began to curse her with words that cannot even be found in the mouth of the worst person on the earth. There are no words to express how small she felt. She sat up, holding her head in her hands. She realized Satan had kicked her in the face and in the back of her head. The kicks were so swift she didn't even see them coming. She just found herself on the floor.

Lisa realizes there are others inside the room besides herself and Satan when she hears them laughing at her. Slowly she looks up and sees three figures seated at the conference table. One looked like a huge Python. Another slim, almost as handsome as Satan, was dressed in what seemed to be an ambassador's outfit. He was representing a particular area and came to report his progress. Lisa noticed he was seated in the first seat. That was the seat Kingpin wanted. When Lisa recognized who it was, she doubted if Kingpin would ever gain that seat of honor. He might sit in the second seat for a long time but she didn't think he would ever be seated in seat number one.

She knew that the Spirit of Greed, as he was called, had that place of honor since the fall of Adam and Eve. There was no way he would give up that seat. As a matter of fact, Kingpin worked for Greed. Greed didn't work for him. Lisa realizes now what the ruling spirit over Halal is. It is the Spirit of Greed. The other spirits are his first officers. The first officers have other spirits working for them. The third spirit is the Spirit of Intellect and it works very closely with Greed and Kingpin. It has people thinking they are not vulnerable. Those that think this are in their demonic grip. The Spirit of Intellect occupies the third seat.

Kingpin is not in on this meeting. He is back on earth watching the home of Karen Kingslei. He is not needed in this conference. Satan has already conferred with him.

Satan, seated at the head of the table, speaks. "The meeting is now called to order. " Lisa sits on the floor, away from them, but they make sure she hears every word. It involves family, especially her Cousin Maria.

She trembles in great fear of what they have planned for her. They also discuss her mother and the Greens. They are referred to as "troublemakers".

Satan tells Python, "You are to squeeze the life from Maria, invade her dreams, appear to her in her drug-induced highs and speak to her. When she is asleep, awaken her suddenly with your body wrapped around her. Convince her you are her friend. Convince her to obtain a Python for a pet. That is your open door to begin to possess her. She has switched to the drugs LSD and Meth which will alter her mind dramatically.

Intellect, that is when you will come in. You know that this is a very intellectual family. Most of them have a lot of book knowledge but they have abused it, thanks to you. That family as a whole has stopped listening to Karen and gone after their own gods thanks to us. We give them a little knowledge, a little money and they serve us. Isn't it funny that they think they are well off financially and mentally? If they only knew. By earth's standards, they are financially secure and very intelligent but their intelligence comes straight from the pit of hell.

The higher Maria gets on PCP, the more it will cause her to have great visions, give her great sayings, and allow her to maintain her grades in school. All the time, Python will be slowly eating away at her brain cells. This will not be noticeable to Maria. She will think she has done something that Lisa could not do. She will feel she is better equipped to handle the drugs whereas Lisa could not. Let her believe this fallacy. She will think she is immune. She will think death is far from her. Intellect, play with her mind. Take over her will and emotions completely. I want the four of you to deliver Maria into Death's hands as soon as possible; because I want KAREN KINGSLEI AND THE GREENS out of my hair! Do you understand me? They bow their heads in respect and say all together, "Yes master, we understand." They do not like it when Satan gets angry. They never know what he might do to them. And they definitely do not want to lose rank.

Satan looks at Intellect long and hard. Then he speaks. He tells Intellect, "I want her to die a tormenting death. I want Mrs. Kingslei to see it. I want Maria to go completely out of her mind before she dies. I want all of this to take place in front of Mrs. Kingslei. Do you understand me?" Intellect nods knowingly.

Greed, you are to supervise everything that takes place. Give them full range to do all they need to do but be there to give help where it is needed.

You know Maria likes money and nice things. You also know what you have to do. I do not need to repeat my orders to you. Just do what you did in the garden. Women are the same all over. Just tell her she can become a queen in her own right. Intellect will have her thinking she is as smart as the God of the universe. Oh, how I hate Him. But He won't be God long. I will win the final war. They all say, "Amen." But Satan states "Let's all get back to the subject at hand. Greed, whisper to her as often as you can. Tell her she is equal to a queen. Are there any questions? If not, you Spirits may head for earth and join Kingpin. He already has two imp types with him. They are just workers. They do not think. Leave them with Kingpin."

As they leave the conference table, they walk up to Lisa. Greed informs her that her little cousin will be joining her soon. Lisa dare not open her mouth for fear of reprisal from the enemy. In Lisa's mind, she is thinking Maria has at least 4 years on earth because this plan needs four years of earth time to work well and Satan didn't tell them to have her in Hell at a specific time.

Lisa thinks maybe, just maybe, Maria will have time to go in the other direction and not in this direction. She will need help. How can I help her? Satan looks at Lisa and dismisses her to head back to her place of torment. There was guard at the door ready to escort her.

As she gets up to leave, Satan tells Lisa, "You cannot help her. There isn't any help for her."

Lisa thinks to herself (forgetting Satan can read her every thought), "He is a genius but he is crazy." Satan throws his head back and roars with laughter at that thought. Then he dismisses her once again.

Back in her place of torment, Lisa looks and sees her two tormentors. Something seemed out of the ordinary. They did not approach her to torment her. They were very quiet. They seem terrified. Lisa looked around. She didn't notice anything different.

She looked towards earth and saw the spirits around her old living quarters back on earth. She saw her mother and Marie sitting on the couch in the living room. She saw the Holy Spirit but decided not to try to engage Him in conversation. She knew it would be futile.

* * * * *

All of a sudden, Lisa looked in another direction. Her gaze went farther than the earth. She looked higher and higher. She could not believe her eyes. She was looking into the very throne room of God. It made Satan's throne room look like an average room. It made his throne room look quite common. The colors there were colors that Satan couldn't even copy. They were beautiful. She sucked in a deep breath. She saw God the Father of Heaven and Jesus seated upon their thrones and holding a conversation. She couldn't hear what they were saying but she was in awe at their appearance.

Lisa thought, "Well, I might as well not even try to talk to them. If the Holy Spirit wouldn't answer me, neither will they." Lisa looked around at her two spirits again and saw they still had not moved.

Lisa decided to try and talk with Jesus or His Father. What did she have to lose? Lisa cried out, "Will one of you answer me? I have questions. The Spirit upon the earth will not answer. Will one of you answer me?" She waited to hear a voice from heaven. She didn't have to wait long. The voice answered her and all Hell stood still and trembled. They recognized the voice of the one who defeated them in their own territory. Lisa's tormentors fell on their faces then screamed and cried, "Leave us alone, Jesus. Why must you talk with her? You do not belong here. Leave us." Lisa fell on her face, afraid of what would happen.

Jesus asked Lisa why she called Him? He told her she had chosen her destiny. She had chosen her god whom she would serve throughout eternity. What did she want with Him?

When the two spirits realized Jesus was talking to Lisa and was not going to bother them; they stood up but they were very quiet. They stood in a dark corner hoping He would not look in their direction with those eyes of His.

Very slowly, Lisa stood up, hoping He would not knock her down. Here she was comparing Him to Satan. She never knew what Satan would do to her. And she was never prepared for the onslaughts from him. With Jesus, she did not have any idea what He would do to her. After all, she had not chosen to serve Him.

Lisa realized she was still standing. She also knew Jesus was awaiting an answer from her. Lisa spoke slowly. "Why won't the Holy Spirit answer my questions?" she asked Jesus. "Why does He ignore me? I have so many questions for Him." When Lisa had finished, Jesus spoke, "He owes you nothing. He does not have to answer you now. When He tried, over your earthly years, to talk with you and keep you out of trouble and keep danger from crossing your path; you mocked Him, cursed Him and told Him you didn't want anything to do with Him. When you spoke those words to the Holy Spirit to leave you alone, when you told Him you did not want Him; His presence left you forever. With that you left yourself open for full possession of demonic activity and for death to take you at his will and time. What is left for the Holy Spirit to say to you?"

Lisa replied, "But I have so many questions for Him." Jesus tells her, "He will not furnish you with any answers." Again Lisa asks, "But why?" Jesus reiterated, "His ministry is to those on the earth, not in hell. You do not have need for Him to minister to you. To Him, you are lost so He will not waste His time with you. He is out to help those who allow Him to do so. As far as He is concerned, you do not exist. If you had chosen heaven, He would have rejoiced. You did not and He cannot take time to weep. There are too many souls left to snatch out of Hell's fire before it is too late. Lisa, there isn't anything left for Him to say to you. You are a damned spirit forever."

Lisa begins to weep and wail, "Why me? I'm too young to be here". Jesus answers her, "Why you? It was your choice. You knew what to do. You had some idea of how to pray. You knew what the Bible was for. You chose not to read it. You chose not to pray. It was a decision of your own will." With that answer, Lisa remembers a scripture her mother used to say to her if she did not change her masters "….In Hell you shall lift your eyes…" Lisa's mother would paraphrase Luke 16:23. What Lisa remembers most about that quotation is that her mother was not using it as a weapon against her; she only wanted Lisa to think about what she was doing to herself.

Lisa was about to ask Jesus another question when Satan arrived on the scene. He interrupted her with his own question, "Why are you talking to Him? I can answer any anything you want to know. I can show you whatever you desire to see. You are here with me now. I am your master." With that answer to Lisa, he stopped to see what Jesus would reply. Jesus never said one word. He knew what Satan said to Lisa was true. He is Lisa's master in hell. Jesus looked at Lisa and wept. He told her she did not have to be in that place of torment. It was not meant for human spirits. But, if humans choose to serve Satan as their god, when they leave their bodies; in hell, they will be with their father, the devil.

After that reply, Jesus went back and sat upon His throne and continued His conversation with His Father.

* * * * *

Satan turns and leaves Lisa's area. He did not look in her direction. He knew she was his to do whatever he wanted with, whenever he wanted. He felt great satisfaction. He knew what Lisa would have done to his kingdom if she had chosen to serve his enemy.

Lisa sat in her dark, little corner crying and cursing. She hated hell and all it stood for. Suddenly, she saw herself at the age of 14, sitting on her bed (the same bed she died on).

She began to reminiscence about her conversation with God about the weather that day. It was a summer storm - thunder and lightning. The wind was blowing. But for some strange reason, to Lisa that storm was extraordinary. To her, it seemed different than most summer storms. She looked out the window up into the sky and knew God and she were having a conversation about her life's work.

She had promised God that if He wanted her to be a missionary on foreign fields, she would. She told God whatever He wanted her to do she would do. Whatever He wanted her to be, she would be to the best of her ability. She prayed and asked Him to help her and be her guide. To keep danger and harm out of her way. To give her His wisdom about different situations. To give her angels to be with her and warn her of dangerous situations and about the wrong company. She told God she wanted to be a lawyer to follow in her father's footsteps but, if He wanted her to be a missionary, she would be that.

What Lisa did not realize was that the Spirit of Intellect was hiding in the corner of her room to go and report to Satan. She did not realize that, not only was God hearing her prayer, so was the devil's spy.

As she reminiscences, she sees where she made her mistake. She started listening to the spirit of intellect and she entertained his thoughts. She believed it was her thoughts to go to college and study law. She convinced herself it would be alright with God. Lisa entered graduate school at age 19. She skipped two grades because she was super intelligent. Lisa's birthday was September 3rd. She was in grad school for two months and died.

As Lisa looked back over her life on earth, she thinks to herself how selfish a person she was. What a promising life she had ahead of her if she had only listened to her mother. Again, she thought, "20 years old was too young to die." Then she said out loud, "But I am not dead. I am alive to live in this hellish torment forever, for an eternity."

Lisa saw that Power and Prince of Night were standing very close to her. She wondered what they were getting ready to do to her. They just stood and looked down at her. Then they stooped down and looked very closely into her eyes. They said to each other, "There's no need to bother with her. She is tormented just seeing the little bit about her past that she looked at in this short period." Prince of Night said to Power, "The strategy we can use to torture her is to repeatedly let her see her life back on earth. But show it to her when she does not expect to see it and make her view it."

This gave them great pleasure. They looked at her and let out howls that caused all the other demons, devils and unnatural life forms to join in. It did not do any good to try to cover her ears. There was no way she could escape the roaring.

* * * * *

Greed, Intellect, Kingpin and Python made their way into Maria's bedroom. There they awaited her arrival. Karen

Kingslei became very alarmed in her spirit. Something very chilling just entered into her home. She heard the Holy Spirit speaking to her. He told her to call her friend, Leali, tell her what she just felt and have her come over this way. She would have someone to help her in intercessory prayer. He told her this is a very serious matter; that Satan had sent four of his strongest spirits of darkness to try and destroy her household.

Karen immediately began to pray, asking God the name of the spirits she would be dealing with. Still praying, she picked up the phone and called Leali. She told Leali everything she had picked up on in her spirit. Leali told her they would pray to God in his throne room in the third Heaven. She told Karen they certainly needed to know the names of those spirits. Leali said it would not be an easy task but it could be done.

While Karen was talking to Leali on the phone, Maria became agitated. She let out a loud sigh. She stood up, stretched and headed upstairs toward her bedroom. Of course, this pleased the spirits that were stationed in her bedroom.

As Maria sat on her bed, the spirit of Intellect whispered into her ears, "Ask your Aunt Karen for Lisa's old bedroom. It is a lot larger than yours and you will have more room and a lot more light coming through the window." Maria was in deep thought. It sounded like a good idea but how would her aunt like the idea? After all, Lisa was her baby, the love of her life. Intellect became persistent. "Ask her now!", he insists.

Maria gets off her bed and moves towards the stairs. She leans over the railing and sees her aunt sitting on the couch still talking on the phone. Maria feels sick to her stomach. "All this talk about Jesus and all this praying makes me sick", she mumbles to herself. Maria called to her aunt. "Aunt Karen", she repeats, "May I speak to you please?" Karen excuses herself from her conversation. She looks in Maria's direction and asks, "What is it?" Maria answered, "Would it be alright with you if I moved my things into Lisa's old room? It is much more spacious than the middle bedroom and I could use the extra space." Karen paused, looked up at Maria then gave her consent.

Maria thanked her aunt then headed back into her room to prepare for her move. She gathered all of her clothing and took them into the back bedroom. It took about an hour to move all of her belongings into her new bedroom. After she settled in, she stretched across the bed and thought about Lisa. That was encouraging to Intellect. He told her she would not make the same mistakes Lisa made. He told her she was much more intelligent than her cousin. Maria smiled at the thought and dosed off into a deep sleep.

Python moved into position to begin his maneuvering in her mind. His first attack is just a dream of himself. She sees a very large snake in her sleep. What's strange is that the snake was flesh toned. It had the color of a human being. When she saw this, she awakened with a start. After getting herself together, she relaxed and thought, "What a strange dream."

Python suggests to her, "Get a pet snake. They are so much fun. You don't have to do much for them and they are quite harmless." Maria shudders at the thought. She decides it is time for a fix. After her fix, Python moves in as Satan had commanded him to do. As Maria's mind is opened more to the spirit world, Python has everything he needs to work with. He wraps himself around Maria, beginning at her feet. He does this so his face is in front of hers and she will never forget what he looks like.

As he moves up and around, his grip tightens until reaches Maria's face. He pauses and stares at her. She, in return, stares back at him. All the while, his grip is tightening. But Maria is so spaced out that she doesn't realize what he is doing. She thinks she is having a vision about a huge snake. He speaks to her. He tells her again to buy a snake. "It will be good for your psyche", he tells her as she stares into the serpent's eyes. "You will have great thoughts and such great visions."

Meanwhile, Python slowly eases his way into her forehead. He maneuvers himself to completely take up all the space in her will, mind and emotions. Maria is still assuming it is a vision. As Python wraps himself around Maria's brain, he bites into areas of the brain that control the will and intellect. When he disengages, he is pleased to see her swaying to and fro in a serpentine manner. He thinks to himself, "I have done a fine job on this one."

He continues the biting over the length of her body as his spirit is infused into Maria.

He moves back into a corner of the room to observe his effect on her spirit. As she sways to the infusion of his spirit, he marvels at her acceptance of his spirit. When she awakens from her sleep, she continues flowing under the influence of his spirit. Shortly, she dresses and departs with Intellect following.

* * * * *

Lisa is watching this unbelievable scenario from the pit of Hell. She thinks to herself, "What an ingenious plot of my master. He is so deceptive. If Maria is not careful she will lift up her eyes in hell. I see now that I can't help her. I have problems of my own. The only help on earth is my mother and the Greens. Anyway, she has plenty of time; she is still very young. Satan has no need of her at the moment."

Lisa's throat is parched. She is so thirsty. Her whole body seems to be on fire. She asked her two spirits for water to drink. That was hilarious to them. They laughed and laughed. Prince of Night stopped suddenly and looked at her. He said, "So you're thirsty and want a drink of water? If you can find water here in hell, you may have it." With that answer, he laughed again. Power was rolling on the floor laughing hysterically. He looked at Prince of Night and repeated his words. "If she can find water, she can have it. Oh, that is amusing", he said.

Then he stopped laughing and looked at Prince of the Night. He had something in his hand and was moving towards Lisa. When he reached her, he told her to stand up. He told her he had something for her to drink. He handed her a vessel containing something that looked like jagged-edged, hot coals with foaming liquid around it. The liquid resembled lava, similar to what she received when she entered Hell for the first time.

Power smiled as Prince handed Lisa the liquid. Prince told her to drink it, saying it would soothe her parched throat. As she hesitated, Prince reiterated, "It will cool your dry, parched throat. Your mouth is so dry. Well, drink this and be happy." As Lisa looked into the vessel, she noticed the lava was boiling over onto her hands. The pain was excruciating. Power said to Lisa, "Drink it now or suffer our wrath."

Lisa put the vessel to her mouth and started

drinking the liquid. With every mouthful, she screamed in agonizing pain. Prince told her not to pull the vessel from her mouth until he gave the word. So Lisa drank and drank. It seemed to go on forever. But then she thought, "What is forever? There isn't any time in hell. Eternity is simply forever."

Finally, Prince of the Night told her to stop. Lisa put the vessel in his hand and he immediately smashed it into her face. He told her not to make a sound. He told her to suffer like the woman she thought she was back on earth. With that, he and Power moved into their private area. They began to talk in their hellish language. Lisa could not understand them. She realized they spoke in this language when they were conspiring against her or talking about secrets of Hell.

* * * * *

Lisa looked up toward heaven. She saw Jesus walking by what looked like a crystal clear lake. He was talking with her father. They stopped and put their feet in the water. She looked closer and saw them sit down and swing their feet in the water. They were laughing and talking. Lisa thought, "Oh, they seem to be having so much fun. If only I could have some of that cool water."

Jesus turned His attention towards Lisa. He knew she was looking at them. Jesus just looked at her. His eyes looked so sad and hurt. His whole expression had changed when he looked upon her. Her father was also looking at her with the same expression. After her father looked for a while, he got up and left. He had to go about his business and continue on his journey for he had an assignment to fulfill in the timeframe set in heaven.

Jesus knows Lisa's thoughts and he comments, "Heavens water will not go into Hell. For the two will not touch and agree. What belongs in Hell is Hell's and what belongs in Heaven is Heaven's."

Lisa responded, "But I am so thirsty." Jesus replied, "And you shall be for an eternity." Jesus told Lisa, "My Father had such great plans for you. You were an instrument He would have used to snatch souls out of hell's fire and instead you chose to be a member of Hell's society. So, all that belongs to Hell's society is also a part of your heritage. It was your choice."

Lisa asked Jesus, "What would it have been like if I had made the right choice?" Jesus told her the anointing upon her would have been awesome. She would have operated in the gift of faith to do whatever the Holy Spirit told her to do at any given time. He told her that her prayer life would have made the very foundation of Hell shake and Heaven rejoice. He told her she would have learned the art of prayer. She would have been able to pray for any need, great or small. It would not matter because her love for God and people would have been without measure.

Lisa asked, "But what happened to me?" Jesus answered, "You know what happened. You allowed the Spirit of Greed and Selfishness to take over your life. At first, you did not know who they were. When you asked the Holy Spirit to help you, He did. He showed you both of those spirits but, when you decided to live your own life, you paid the price for it. He was there until you told Him to leave you alone.

Jesus told Lisa he had to leave for He had work to do. With that He walked in the same direction her father had taken.

* * * * *

ack on earth, Maria is still high. She continues her walk and Intellect walks side by side with her. He is leading her in the direction of the pet store. Maria believes she just needs a breath of fresh air so she walks on, heading where, she couldn't tell you. She did not have the foggiest notion to where she was walking. She started to come down from her high slowly as she walked. Intellect talked to her about her vision. He told her to do what she heard the serpent say - purchase the Python. It would talk to her and give her great wisdom. Maria thought, "This is a perfect idea." I will show everyone that I am smarter than Lisa was. Before she knew it, she was in front of the pet shop.

Maria looked into the window for a few seconds. Then she remembered, "I don't have my purse with me." Intellect interjected, "They will hold it for you. Go inside." Maria entered the pet shop. As she looked around all she saw were puppies, kittens and other small creatures but not one snake.

She started to walk out but decided to ask the person behind the counter if they had any snakes. He told her they usually did not keep snakes but they had a recent acquisition. Someone could no longer keep their snake as a pet and wanted the pet shop to help them sell it to a good home. Maria asked what kind of snake it was and was told it was a Python. It was a female, about six months old. The clerk asked if she would be interested in seeing it. Maria said she would so he directed her to a back room area.

As soon as Maria looked at the snake, it looked at her and moved closer to the glass enclosure. Maria thought the look she received was familiar but then dismissed the thought. She asked for the price. Then she remembered her vision. She remembered seeing the eyes. She thought, "This is great." She told the owner of the shop, "I want that snake. Don't sell it. I'll be right back with the cash."

Intellect was pleased with the transaction. Her next question to herself was where she would be able to keep the snake so her aunt would not easily locate it and have one of her fits - telling her about Jesus and how the snake represents evil or that man and snakes are natural enemies. Her aunt would lecture her about how God put enmity between man and the serpent in the Garden after the fall of man. She did not want to hear any of that nonsense. After all, she had just had a great revelation about that particular snake.

Intellect just chuckled. He knew those were his words to Maria. Of course, she is thinking how intelligent she is becoming. Now, where to put her pet? It suddenly came to her. Aunt Karen doesn't go down into the basement. That would be an ideal hideout for her pet.

Maria walked into the house and immediately went to her room. She did not want to face her aunt. She could not look into her aunt's eyes any longer. Those eyes were like fire burning straight through her. She hated that. Maria was starting to despise her aunt and she could not understand why. She remembered all that her Aunt Karen had done for her and was continuing to do for her; but still she felt this uncontrollable hatred for her.

What Maria didn't understand was that she was becoming possessed by spirits of darkness. Even her room was kept in darkness, even in daylight or with the lights turned on. But Maria could not see this. It was spiritual warfare. A fight for her very spirit was taking place. Maria sat on her dressing chair and looked into the mirror noting her eyes looked different.

But she thought, "This is good. I am starting to resemble a person of infinite knowledge and wisdom. I can see into the future and know what has happened in the past, while being aware of what is going on in the present."

Python moved over to the chair and slowly started to ease himself into her body, mind and spirit. He allowed her to see him. He again bit her all over. It was so painful but he told her it was important for her to suffer because suffering brings on great knowledge. So she gave him permission to continue.

Because she wanted this knowledge, she held back her screams. But Maria had no idea what was in store for her. This time he did not leave. He possessed her completely. He had taken up residence inside of her being. The pain was so great. Kingpin told Maria to take something for the pain so she injected some LSD.

The combination of the pain and the drugs

put Maria on a wild trip. She saw her cousin in her torturing place crying out to Maria to stop and save herself. She saw cats which were part human. And she saw large, ugly bats with sharp, canine-like teeth and claws that looked like they were on human legs. They resembled the creatures that were presently torturing her cousin in Hell. She also saw a person sitting on a throne smiling and looking in her direction. "He is quite handsome", she thought.

The two creatures dragged Lisa into the room before the person sitting on the throne. They threw her at his feet. He began kicking and beating her until he was satisfied. Maria began laughing hysterically and couldn't seem to stop. Karen heard the laughter and ran upstairs into Maria's room. Usually she did not enter Maria's room without knocking; but this time she did. What she saw shocked her.

Maria was writhing on the floor and she was totally uncontrollable. There were marks on her body which appeared to be some kind of teeth marks. Karen saw all of the evidence of drug abuse and began weeping for her niece.

Karen started to help Maria up from the

floor. As she did this, Maria wrapped her arms around her and began to squeeze her aunt uncontrollably. Karen was unable to break free from this grip. Karen began to pray out loud asking God for strength. While doing this, she heard her spirit cry out for the Blood of Jesus knowing this would cause Maria to release her. Karen Kingslei spoke in a clear, powerful, strong voice; "Satan, the Blood of Jesus is against you and I have immunity in the Blood of Jesus. Now release me!"

With those words, Maria released her and cowered in a corner of the room. Karen looked at her niece and knew she was dealing with something even greater than what she had dealt with in Lisa. Karen learned something about herself also. She realized she had gained greater spiritual insight than ever before. She saw something she had never seen before when she called upon the Blood of Jesus. This was very new to Karen. She loved this newfound strength. She thought to herself, "I will not lose this war. God, give me more insight about what I have in you." Then Karen received this response in her spirit, "Read my Book and learn of me. Listen to how I tell you to pray. Just follow my instructions."

Karen walked over to Maria and told her to get off the floor. Maria hissed at her aunt, her eyes resembling a serpent's eyes. Karen, in a firm voice said, "I have immunity in the Blood of Jesus." Maria jumped off the floor, grabbed her purse and ran screaming loudly from the house. When she was a safe distance from the house, Python calmed down. When he relaxed, Maria began to appear normal again. She, of course, could not remember any of what had just happened.

Walking slowly, she headed for the pet shop to purchase her snake. Maria glanced at her arms and legs noticing what appeared to be teeth marks all over her limbs. She paused for a closer look at the marks then thought about her vision. She said to herself, "Are these just visions or am I opening up a link with the spirit realm so I can have greater, more powerful thoughts?"

Meanwhile, in her dining room, Karen is impressed to pray while remembering what the Holy Spirit had spoken to her while dealing with the spirit in Maria. She stopped setting the table and began to pray. For some reason, she thought she had a vision of what looked like a snake in the back of a pet shop.

She knew there were no snake sales in the pet shop in Halal' but she decided to pray anyway.

She commanded the snake to die in the Name of her Jesus and covered herself with immunity in His Blood. She told the spirit it would not possess her household nor come near her dwelling. She appropriated Psalm 91 and loosed the angels to be in charge of the situation, to protect all that she had and to be a guard around her. Karen cursed that spirit. She still did not know its name but she was getting results. The pet python died for what appeared to be no apparent reason. After she prayed, she continued setting the table for dinner.

When Maria reached the pet shop, she was advised the snake had suddenly died and that he would not be obtaining any more snakes of any type. When Maria asked why not, the clerk advised her there would be no further purchase of exotic pets. He told her they were too much trouble and the level of care needed is more than they could provide. He reminded her how he had obtained the snake in the first place. Maria left the store. She decided she was intelligent enough and didn't really need the hassle of a pet in the first place.

Python was highly annoyed with Karen. He had picked up on her prayers but, knowing how she used to pray, he wasn't worried. But this prayer was different. Then he remembered what had just happened in Maria's bedroom. He recognized her prayers were different and more powerful. He wondered if his master knew about the change in Karen Kingslei's prayer life. Then he decided he would not be the one to inform him. Let someone else suffer his wrath.

This was one time Python was glad his master is not omnipresent. He directed Maria back to her residence because he needed to have a conference with the spirit of greed.

* * * * *

Lisa decided to look toward heaven in hopes of seeing God. She realized her eyes were looking at something quite different. She saw an altar made of pure gold. It was quite large and so beautiful. But what was truly amazing was that on the altar was a fountain of pure gold. Out of the fountain, instead of water, flowed blood. It never stopped its flow down then up and back into the fountain. It never touched the edge or fell on the floor and made perfect music in its own rhythm. It was so beautiful, such a sweet sound of its own. As she listened, she heard a song coming from the Blood.

She had never seen anything like it. She had seen beautiful water fountains before at different occasions, but nothing as exquisite as the fountain that contained the Blood of Jesus. Oh, how it sparkled. She saw God of the heavens looking toward the earth. He would always remember the work that Jesus had done and continue to forgive and give the human voice a chance toward salvation. The God of the Heavens said out loud, "Oh man, born of a woman, you don't have very long. Soon the end will come and I will judge the sins of you and your children and your children's children."

Lisa knew all that the Bible said about the Blood of Jesus was true. No wonder Satan and all his cohorts hate it so. The Blood is alive and powerful. Lisa did not see Jesus so she decided not to ask God-Jesus-The Father any questions.

* * * * *

erry and Leali Green arrived at Karen's house for dinner. After the meal, Karen told them about the encounter and how the Spirit of God told her to pray. She told them about how she had seen the snake in the pet shop and how she had told it to die. Karen provided them with full details about everything.

Jerry and Leali just looked at her. Then Jerry spoke. He told her that somehow Satan had intended for some type of snake to come into her dwelling in the natural and in the spirit. He told her the war was not over yet. He warned that she must continue to do warfare against the enemy. He sensed in his spirit that she had stopped the snake from coming into the house in the natural; but something was definitely wrong in the spirit realm.

Leali asked Karen if anything strange had occurred in her home. Karen remembered the encounter with Maria and gave them the details about it, including how she even looked and acted like a serpent.

They all stated it at the same time, "This is it." The spirit of a snake had taken over Maria. That is how it intended to come into your home. They agreed the only thing Karen could do for Maria was to pray for her. You can't go against her will but, through your prayers, God will give her the opportunity to be free from that spirit. Jerry stopped. Then he told Karen, "I believe there are at least three other spirits trying to possess her and they are some of Satan's strongholds. Karen, do not fear or be afraid. They cannot touch you as long as you follow God's instructions for your life. You will win this battle. We will win this city for God and for God it shall be once again."

As the Greens and Karen continued their conversation, the Holy Spirit whispered the word Python into Jerry's ear. Jerry stopped talking to his wife and Karen and asked the Holy Spirit, "What did you say?" The ladies answered, "We didn't say anything; you were talking to us." Jerry responded, "No, not you, the Holy Spirit." The Holy Spirit again said, "Python. It is the spirit of Python that has possessed Maria."

Jerry jumped up and said, "That's it! That's it!!! It's the spirit of Python." He looked at Karen and said, "Now you know its name. Come against the Spirit of Python from now on!"

Karen asked, "How are these spirits coming into our lives? This, I must find out." Jerry said, "The Lord will reveal it to you very soon. Be patient and be brave."

Upstairs in Maria's bedroom, the Spirit of Greed was becoming agitated. He knew something had to be done and it had to be done very quickly. He told Kingpin "Things are not going the way our master planned." Kingpin told Greed, "Well, Mr. Know It All, it's your assignment, not mine. What are you going to do about it?" Greed reached out suddenly and knocked Kingpin clear across the room. Kingpin laughed and said "Yep, you can whip me all you want. But what can you do with the Master?" Greed growled at him. He told Kingpin, "I'd better go and report our progress first. Then I'll tell him the problem. Maybe he won't be too upset." Kingpin said, "Yep sure, if you believe that, I believe in Jesus." Greed told Kingpin to keep his eyes open and his ears tuned in to Karen's prayers and her conversations with the Greens. He was to report back to him when he got back from his meeting with his master, Satan. With that, he headed for the opening to Hell.

* * * * *

A s he entered the gate, heading into the mouth of Hell, he shook with fear. How could he explain what had happened to his master, Satan? He took his time heading for the throne room. When he reached it, he stood at the entrance. He looked around for Satan but did not see him. Suddenly, he felt a hand on his back. He jumped in surprise when he saw it was his master. He bowed and worshipped him. "I have news for you." Satan told him to come in and then proceeded to the conference table. When they were seated Satan spoke in a low tone, "So, report. You only come to me in the middle of an assignment when things are going wrong. You'd better not screw up on this project or I will have your head and demote you to the last chair. Maybe this job is too much for you; maybe it is more suited for Kingpin. What do you have to say Greed? It better be what I want to hear." He pounded his hand on the table. "Now talk and talk fast!!!"

Greed started off very slowly and had to make his voice strong because he knew he was in much trouble.

"We are winning Maria but her aunt knows about Python."

"That stupid snake. What did he do wrong?"

"It's Karen. She's praying with more knowledge and is getting answers quicker. That's the problem."

"Has Python fully possessed Maria?"

"Yes he has, Master, but that is not the problem. Kingpin is about to enter her body with the next fix then Intellect will enter with her so-called vision. They will all enter her and completely take over. She is depressed and on LSD. We don't even have to give her flashbacks because she'll be using it on a continuous basis."

"That's all good but Karen is a problem. We must get Maria into Hell sooner than I had planned."

Greed nodded in agreement.

"Increase her dosage of the drug. This is Kingpin's assignment. Relay that message to him. Your part is very simple. You are to supervise. You do not have to possess her. You have given her the desire to want more knowledge than her cousin. You've made her greedy for the natural things in the earth realm. She wants to be brainier than any of her relatives. She will go crazy while believing she is a genius. She will not know what hit her. She *is not greedy for money. She is too far gone to even think in that area. Plus, they are very well off by earth's standards. What is today's date on earth?"*

"On earth, it is December 15th", Greed answered.

Satan repeated the date, "The 15th." Greed shook his head yes.

"You must have her here on her birthday. That will be my birthday present to her and my surprise to Lisa. Remember, her birthday is her homecoming day. You are dismissed!"

* * * * *

reed got up and returned to earth. He met with Kingpin where he relayed the message about his assignment. That pleased him very much. Greed told Kingpin, "Satan, our master, wants Maria home on her birthday." Kingpin looked quite surprised. That is December 21st. Greed replied, "Yes, I know that. Remember you told me facing the Master was my problem. Well, this is your problem. All Python has to do is squeeze but you must do what is important. Get the dosage in her and take her mind. Ha! Ha! Are you up to it, Mr. Know It All?" Kingpin snaps back, "Of course I am! Then I will deliver her into Death's hands and we will escort her into hell. You and Python will have the honor of coming along."

* * * * *

Back in Hell, Lisa looks towards the earth and sees the destruction of Maria. She sees Python inside of her cousin and Kingpin and Intellect getting ready for their day of possession. They are elated because they know the time to take their place in Maria's body and mind is very near.

Lisa screams and cries while pulling out her hair. She has a tantrum like none she has ever had before. Power and Prince of Night watch her from their corner and comment to each other. "What is her problem? At least she will have her own flesh and blood here with her. Why is she so upset? We are good to her." With that, they rolled in laughter. Lisa looked at them laughing at her and began to curse them. She told them to shut up and leave her alone. She said, "You have me. Why do you need my baby cousin? Just shut up and leave me alone!"

Lisa knew it was a mistake but she didn't

care about herself anymore. She knew that there would never be any help for her. She knew she was doomed and she was tired of being careful. She was tired of trying not to upset her tormentors. Maybe later she would feel different about this point and time in eternity; but right now, she didn't care. She thought, "Maybe there is still hope and help for Maria. Oh Jesus in heaven, maybe you can still help my cousin. Send help her way, please."

Power and Prince looked at each other. They knew they could not let Lisa get away with belittling them nor would they. They walked over to her and threw her into another wall. This went on and on. Finally, they threw her into the hot lava that flowed all the time. They held her face down in it. They hollered, "Repent! Maybe we will save you." She told them she was sorry and that she repented. They told her that was not good enough then immersed her whole body into the hot lava and flames that seemingly jumped about. It was so hot. The flames looked alive. As they covered Lisa's body, she screamed. You could hear her screams throughout all of Hell. "Do you repent from wanting to help Maria?" She screamed, "YES! I repent for wanting to help her." Prince picked her up by the scruff of her neck and threw her into the far corner. Power told her to stay there and not move.

Lisa sat in the corner and drew her knees close to her chest so she could rest her head on them. Slowly, she looked up and stared towards Heaven. "Why do I torture myself by looking towards Heaven? I certainly can't get there. Well, at least my father is there and it seems as though my mother will be there. I also have many relatives there but that will not do me any good. I am here in this place of torment. Whether human beings believe it or not, Hell is alive and it does enlarge itself to receive more of the human race. My Master is becoming more creative with handling humans when they get here."

* * * * *

Lisa sees Jesus as He walks in a flower garden. He isn't alone. There are children of all races with Him and he begins to play with them. They are laughing and having such a great time. She did not know Jesus could laugh so heartily. She watched as He played with the children. He rolled on the ground with them. Then He would pick them up and toss them in the air. He was having so much fun.

After the fun and games, He and the children sat down and talked. He would talk and they would listen. Then they would talk to Him and He listened with great interest. Oh, how he loved them! She could see it all in His face and in the way He handled them. He knew what each one wanted and what each one needed. Finally, the children left with some of the adults. Jesus just sat there for a while, smiling, as the children went on their way. He knew Lisa was watching but He did not look in her direction. He got up and started walking. Lisa did not have any idea where he was headed. She called out, "Jesus, may I please have a conference with you?"

Jesus stopped and looked at her. Then He said, "You may have a brief moment. I'm on my way to see my Father. What do you want of me?" Lisa said, "Can you help? You know who I'm talking about. I can't mention the name or I will get my head knocked off my shoulders."

Jesus replied, "Only if she heeds what the

Holy Spirt speaks to her spirit. Then she must do exactly what He tells her to do. Only then, can there be help for her. It is still not too late. As long as there is breath in her physical body there is hope for her."

"This is the last time I will answer any of your questions. This is the last time you will be able to look up into Heaven for there will be put a great cloud which you will not be able to see through. This is your last contact with my Father's kingdom. You will not even see your mother's homecoming. For you are there and she will be here. When this conversation is over, I will not speak to you until the judgement day of the dead. And that will be only to judge you and cast you into the Lake of Brimstone and Fire. You are doomed for eternity." He tells Lisa, "Now my presence will leave you forever. You will not have any more contact with Heaven." With that, the great cloud formed and Lisa was alone with her two evil spirits.

* * * * *

Satan sends for Lisa. Two guards, resembling oversized cats, came for her. They walked upright but they even purred liked cats. They didn't take Prince of Night and Power but they told her to get going. "The Master wants to see you." She walked quietly between the two guards. They made no sounds except to meow and purr to each other. Lisa couldn't understand them but they seemed to understand each other.

They escorted her into Satan's throne room. He is seated upon his throne and can't wait to antagonize Lisa. She gives homage to him. When he tells her to rise, she stands up and faces him. Lisa remains very quiet, waiting to see what her master is up to this time.

"So, how do you like Maria's progress?" Lisa did not comment. Satan, angered by her silence, repeated the question in a louder tone. "I said, how do you like your cousin's progress?" Lisa hesitantly looked at her master for a moment. Then she replied, "Master, Lord Satan I would not wish my worst enemy to come to this place. It seems good for you and your high ranking officers but, for the rest of us, it is exactly what this place is called! It is Hell in the most literal sense. Even some of your workers are tormented so, no, I do not like Maria's progress."

Satan roared with laughter. He told her, "You haven't seen pain yet. Wait until Maria arrives and I pit the two of you against each other. Then you will know pain, great pain. You will have to look at her for an eternity and she will have to look at you."

Lisa asked him to explain what he meant. He told her, "Just wait and see." Lisa looked down at herself. For the first time, she noticed she was still wearing the outfit she had on when she entered Hell, including being barefoot.

Lisa asked Satan, "Why am I still dressed in this manner? Why don't you provide shoes for me? After all, it is hot walking on the coals and lava down here." He informs her that, in Hell, she does not need any other clothing. "As for the shoes, who cares if your feet get burned? After all, your spirit and soul will burn forever. How you entered Hell is how you will remain forever." Lisa looked at Satan and spit at him, which was a mistake. When he jumped suddenly from the throne, she knew he was going to beat the fire out of her. Instead, he just spoke very softly, "Just for that, I WILL TELL YOU Maria's homecoming date. It is on her birthday, December 21st." Satan looked at Lisa as if he dared her to say one word. Wisely, she did not open her mouth as he waved his hand and dismissed her. Lisa bowed and backed out of the throne room with the two guards on either side of her.

Lisa is back in her area. She knows the time for Marie is very short. She tries to think what the date is by earth's standards. There is no time in hell; it just goes on and on. There is no day or night. Just darkness, gloom and heat. Heat is everywhere and there is no relief. She tries to think. "I entered Hell on November 5th and Maria is expected on December 21st. What is the date by earth's time?" She can't remember. Then it hits Lisa like a ton of bricks. She cannot relate any more with earth or heaven, just with hell. Although she can still see earth at times, it is less and less. Her whole world is becoming the confines of Hell. Lisa isn't sure if days have passed or weeks, months or years. She is very confused about the time. Lisa says to herself, "When will the time come that I will no longer be able to see earth?" She knows the time is coming when that will take place.

Lisa moves over into her favorite little corner. When she did this, Prince of Night and Power started tormenting her by showing her what she could have been. They will be doing this more and more. They know to show a human what they could have been and what they could have done once their spirt and soul leaves the body is the worst of all torment.

Lisa realized she was wailing, groaning and screaming. She was doing this more and more. Her screams became very high pitched. She started gnashing her teeth, something she had never done before. Lisa was becoming more and more acclimated to what life is like in Hell. After viewing her past and what could have been her future, Lisa banged her head on the wall as she pulled out her hair. "Oh, it is so dark! Why did I choose Hell? Why didn't I listen to my mother? She told me of this fate. Oh why didn't I listen?"

* * * * *

Back on earth, Karen is praying. She hears in her heart, "Read Jeremiah 9:1." After she finished praying, she immediately got her Bible and read Jeremiah 9:1. When she finished reading, she asked the Holy Spirit what the verse meant and why He had her read that particular verse. While she waited for an answer, she prayed silently. Suddenly, the

Holy Spirit spoke to her. He told her that her Intercession would rise to another level. He was making her an Intercessor for the young people who were being lost to Satan at such an alarming rate. He told her the meaning of the verse.

The Holy Spirit told Karen, from that moment on, whenever she interceded; she would weep for souls as the verse had said. He told her it would be as though she was the mother of all for whom she prayed. That is what the verse would mean to her. She would be weeping for her spiritual children. That is when light came on her and the words seemed to jump off the pages at her. Now she understood. She thanked the Holy Spirit for entrusting her with that kind of responsibility.

In the meantime, Maria is out partying with friends. Any kind of drug she desires is at this party. Maria had been dancing for hours. She is really up. She feels invulnerable to any kind of harm. Maria is unaware of Kingpin and Intellect's presence; let alone that Python had possessed her.

Someone came over to Maria while she was on the dance floor and tapped her on the shoulder. The person whispered into Maria's ear. She excused herself and headed for the bedroom behind the individual who had come for her. When she was in the bedroom, she had knowledge of the different kinds of drugs that interested her. She was told to help herself. She had heard about Ecstasy and decided it was time to try it. Kingpin impressed upon her to take three patches instead of one. She picked the ones that looked like hearts. Within seconds, she was out of it. She had again opened herself up to the spirit world.

Maria left the bedroom. She didn't have any idea where she was going or even who she was. Maria ended up back in the crowded room where the music was blasting and people were still dancing. She stood in the middle of the floor and just stared. Slowly, she turned in one direction and then the other. She had never felt like this, ever. Suddenly, she started jabbering and babbling. To her, it made great sense. Everything Intellect whispered in her ears was repeated. Intellect was just saying words, lots of words-large and small. He put them all together and they meant absolutely nothing. Just phrases that sounded profound.

People stopped dancing to listen to

Maria's great sayings. They oo'd and aah'd at everything she said. They loved the great words and great sayings. Maria went on for hours. She couldn't stop. The words kept coming. What she didn't realize was that she was losing great amounts of brain cells. Also, her brain was slowly beginning to hemorrhage.

Python got in on the act. The old serpent started to squeeze and bite. Maria stopped talking and grabbed her chest. She was having difficulty breathing. After that, she grabbed her head and her face. The partygoers could see drops of blood trickling down her face, arms and neck then began to think the blood looked like pin needle marks. They did not understand what was happening to Maria.

Maria did not realize she was bleeding. All she felt was the pain. Maria grabbed her arms and neck then rubbed her legs as pain coursed through her body. She had never experienced such agony. She screamed, "Oh, my head! My head feels as though it will explode."

People began to leave the party. They felt Maria's screams would alert the neighbors and bring the police to the area. The owner of the party house took Maria into one of the bedrooms and tried to calm her down. They could not hold her as she had become unusually strong for one of such small stature. She had gained supernatural strength.

It was long into the night as different ones tried to get Maria to settle down and possibly go to sleep. She was like a wild maniac. She continued screaming about a snake trying to kill her. Only she could see Python. The others could not see him operating.

She screamed, "STOP!" at the top of her voice. "Stop taking my breath. They said you would be my friend. You are supposed to help me, not hurt me."

Finally, the pain began to lift. Maria came around slowly. After consuming the large amount of drugs, she would never be the same. Maria never realized this would be a revealing repercussion of her actions. She got up to leave and noticed the blood on her clothing. It didn't matter to her. Her head felt as though it belonged to someone else. All she wanted to do was go home and get some sleep. She would not have to worry about classes because it's now Sunday morning. She looked at her watch and knew Aunt Karen had gone to bed and would be asleep by the time she returned home.

Maria laid across her bed and closed her eyes to go to sleep. She slowly opened her eyes only to find herself looking into the eyes of Python. She was paralyzed by the face of her tormentor. She wanted to scream; but the scream remained in her throat. She could not move even her small finger. It all seemed so unreal. It felt like a very strange dream; only she was not asleep. One thing gave her comfort. She was a noted genius and Lisa had not reached that status. Her heart was filled with pride.

Kingpin and Intellect knew it was getting close to the time for Maria's homecoming; so they decided it was time to possess her. First Kingpin went in and then Intellect. Now Maria was fully possessed and would not have a will of her own. It was lost to the three demons who had taken her over and possessed her soul.

While sitting in church, Karen knew something terrible was happening to her niece. Within herself, Karen started rebuking evil spirits. She told them to leave her niece alone. As she continued rebuking them she heard these words, "It's too late. She wants us and we have her. So just stop praying to your God. He can't help you now. And YOU are next." Karen immediately rebuked that lying spirit. She told it, "You Will Never Have Me and as long as there is breath in Maria, it is not too late.

After church service, Karen approached Leali and told her something terrible was taking place with Maria. Leali understood exactly what Karen meant. She had a strong impression that death was very close by but she did not voice this to Karen.

Leali motioned for Karen to head to the Pastor's Office. For a few moments, they sat in complete silence. Then Karen began to cry. When she could, she spoke softly to Leali. Her words were broken and choked. "Leali, I sense that Maria is in very serious trouble and that death is closing in on her. You know, when I close my eyes, I can smell the fragrance of funeral flowers. It has a very distinct odor. It's like being in a funeral parlor. My flesh just crawls at the thought of it. Also, I see the face of the spirit of death. It is horrible. It's dressed in black and the face is like a skeleton. The flesh, if you can call it that, is very pale –

almost invisible. It is just waiting for Maria. And another thing, Leali, just before Lisa died her room was icy cold, for lack of a better word. "Icy cold" is the only phrase I can use to describe the feeling. It was not a normal cold. After she died, the coldness left the room. Leali, tell me, do you think my niece will see her 16th birthday?"

Leali was still searching for the right words when Jerry walked into the office. He knew what was going on because he'd had a night vision about the situation, although he did not understand the entire dream. He knew it was about Maria and that she was in the grip of Hell.

Leali spoke, "I do not know how much time Maria has. She could live a full and prosperous life if she would only change Kingdoms. At the moment, she is only interested in what is good for her. What pleases her. All she is concerned about is her right to make her choice."

"Satan has convinced her that her choices are of no consequence. That her choices will not harm her or anyone else. He has told her of her rights as an individual. If it seems right to her, then it's alright and no one has a right to interfere with her choices. So, if drugs are her choice, then it is alright for her. But what Maria fails to realize is that with every choice, there is a consequence – whether it be good or evil – there is a consequence. But her will is completely gone now, turned over to evil. Before that happened, she still had a chance. She was upright. She knows how to pray. But she chose death instead of life."

"Karen, my dear friend, always remember this; there is still a chance for her to choose life as long as there is a breath of life in her body. All we can do is what we have been doing."

Tears rolled down Leali's face. She looked at her husband. She asked if he had anything to add. He just shook his head. He was so troubled in his spirit. All he could add was, "Satan is moving fast in this assignment."

He told Karen she was definitely a thorn in Satan's side and that everything Satan was throwing at her is to take her eyes off of what God the Father has for her to do. He told her not to stop. "Keep your eyes towards heaven and God will keep you strong for the mission that he has for you. All of the church will continue to lift Maria in prayer. Today, Leali and I will go home with you and talk to Maria. We can only do our part to get her on the right track. If she chooses the right path, it will be her decision and her decision alone."

Karen asked Jerry about the dream he had the night before. He thought for a moment then began to describe the dream. "In the dream, there was a great blizzard and Maria was lost in the storm. She was trying to find her way home. I could see Karen standing at the front door and looking out at the storm. You were looking for Maria. You said within yourself that you hoped she would not go out into the storm.

The wind was furious and the snow blew in all directions. You could not see anything, not even your hand if you held it up in front of you. But you knew Maria had gone into the storm and was lost. She was trying to get on the right path to get home but she could not get her bearings. Everything looked the same…just snow and winds everywhere.

In the dream, Maria never did get on the right path but you were still standing by the door, looking out a window for her. Then I was suddenly awakened from the dream. It was one dream of which I was not fond. But one thing we know – the Spirit of God warns us ahead of time so we can do something about it."

Intellect started clawing at Maria's soul. He was causing great pressure and distress. Kingpin put pressure on her body through all of the hits she had taken. Maria was in torment. She did not know where she was, who she was, how to get home or if this was her home.

Intellect clawed and talked, talked and clawed. Python squeezed and bit. She continually heard cynical laughter. It was Kingpin. All of a sudden, she saw the front door of her home. Kingpin allowed her to see it. He told her to run. "Run for your life!" And she did. He pointed her in the right direction of her home.

Maria took off running. She looked like a bolt of lightning. She seemed driven by a supernatural power. Maria had never moved that fast before. Never! She did not like to run. She thought running was not very feminine.

Maria still doesn't realize her shoes are missing. She is running wildly; still hearing the voices of Kingpin and Intellect and still feeling the assault from Python. Maria is screaming loudly. This alarmed the neighbors to the point they began calling the police to report a young woman is being killed somewhere in the area. The calls were coming from multiple blocks as Maria continued running through the area.

Maria lived about a mile from Candice. She left her car parked in front of Candice's house. She is now about a block from home. Kingpin pointed the house out to her as she got closer to the safety of her home. Maria ran onto the porch and pounded on the front door. All three spirits are screaming insults at her. As she is being bombarded with insults, she covers her ears. The effort is futile.

What Maria fails to realize is that the words are coming from inside of her and she cannot block out the words by covering her ears. Somehow, she remembers her aunt's name and frantically calls out to her. "Aunt Karen, PLEASE help me! I'm dying! Please Help Me!! My demons are killing me. Please tell them to STOP!!"

Her voice trails off. Her words become

unintelligible. She is speaking as loud as she can, trying to drown out the voices.

By now, Karen has swung open the front door and, upon seeing Maria, she lets out a loud gasp. Maria pushed past her aunt screaming, "NO, NO, Leave Me Alone! Jesus, don't look at me." The only person looking upon her at the time was her Aunt Karen; but Maria saw the Spirit of God inside of Karen. Just as Maria was possessed with demons, her aunt is possessed with the Holy Spirit of God.

Karen turns around and sees Maria spinning around in circles on the floor. Her eyes are darting back and forth. She looks like she is speaking to someone but there is no one there. But if you understand the spirit realm, you know she sees something or someone.

Karen closed her front door. She started to pray but the Holy Spirit reminded her of what He had spoken to her the day before. He also reminded her that the spirits could not harm her. That, in fact, they are afraid of her. The Holy Spirit tells Karen to call Jerry and Leali as well as 911 emergency. Karen did exactly what the Holy Spirit told her to do.

Death and Greed left the bedroom and

proceeded downstairs into the living room, enjoying the scene before them. They were so gleeful. They began chanting and singing to Satan and the other spirits joined in.

Jerry and Leali arrived just in time to hear Maria uttering this chant to Satan. The words were not clear; but they knew it was demonic.

Suddenly Python stopped chanting and launched an all-out attack on Maria. He viciously bit into her brain and squeezed like he had never done in the past.

Maria is now bleeding from her mouth and nose. She falls onto the floor as if she is having convulsions. Scratches appear on her face, arms, and neck. This is from Intellect and Kingpin. She begins choking on her own blood. Maria has torn her clothing and is crying out desperately, "They are killing me!!!" Kingpin punches her in the stomach which causes her to hemorrhage even more. Now Kingpin gives her his final blow and throws her into the wall.

Slowly, Maria's life is draining from her and death moves in closer. Maria lets out one last loud scream at death, "No, you can't have me. Aunt Karen, Satan lied to me. These spirits are working for him. He doesn't love me. You do, Aunt Karen. You love me". Those were her last words.

The paramedics have arrived and they told Karen they had never seen anyone overdose like this before. As they begin to examine Maria, they suddenly tell Karen there are still signs of life. Just as they say this, Python takes a final, deadly bite which causes Maria's brain to explode as his final squeeze causes her heart to burst. Kingpin was pleased. Death moved in and called Maria by name. She could not resist. Her spirit leaped from her body. Maria is officially dead. Greed moves over next to Death and whispers, "Congratulations!" Python, Kingpin and Intellect left her spirit and stood with the others.

The paramedics told Karen, "She's dead." The time of Maria's death is 11:15 pm. It is still the night of her birthday. Karen couldn't cry. She was in shock. Jerry and Leali stared at Maria's lifeless body…the destruction of another human being. They knew something must be done or this world would experience a generation lost to Satan.

Death looked very long and hard at Maria. Then he told her to follow him. Maria tried to resist. She tried to reenter her body but that was impossible. Death was in full control. There was not a person able to call her back into the natural realm because Maria had chosen her destiny when she chose to allow her body to be possessed by "her demons" as she had often referred to them.

Death stood on one side and Greed stood on the other as they took her by the arms and steered her. They headed towards the entrance of Hell. It was in the same location in the backyard where Lisa had entered. Kingpin, Intellect and Python followed. Death informed Maria that Lisa had gone to her home through the same doorway.

Maria is screaming at the top of her lungs, "Oh God in Heaven, whom my aunt serves; forgive me and have mercy on me. I see the truth now. You are God of the universe. I was wrong. Have mercy on me, a young fool of fools. It can't be too late." Greed angrily slaps her and yells, "Shut up and stop that nonsense! It is too late. You belong to Satan, God of the underworld." He pushed her forward as they descended into Hell which will be her home forever.

After Greed pushed Maria in, he entered. Intellect followed then Kingpin and finally, Python. They were on their way into Hell with their grand prize and all were extremely gleeful. They knew Satan would be very pleased with all of them. Greed knew he would remain in the first chair.

Their conversation is abruptly interrupted by angry words coming at them. It is Maria screaming at the top of her lungs at this procession of spirits. She accuses them of betraying her. She reminded them that they said Hell did not exist. Maria was trying to reach out and claw them. She kept repeating, "You lied to me. You lied to me." She tried to grab Greed but he moved out of reach. Finally, Greed yelled, "I have had enough of this!"

He then grabbed Maria by the arm and told her to shut up and not to say another word. He told her, "You have made your choice. Now you will live with it." She started to reply and he viciously slapped her across the mouth and repeated, "You will shut-up NOW!" Intellect was on the other side of her, Python was in back of her and Kingpin, of course, was in front leading the way.

They continued to descend for approximately six hours – approximately three of those hours were spent in complete silence.

Satan suddenly appears directly in front of Lisa. He seems to be unusually jubilant as he meets with her. Lisa just stares at him. She is being tormented by Satan in the very bowels of Hell. She can't get any relief from the oppressive heat. She thinks to herself, "He wants me to guess what his big surprise is." She looks at her new master and in a cold, strong voice responds, "Master, do me a favor. Get lost!!!" She knew she was there forever and she did not care anymore how she talked to her master. She realized no matter what she did to please him or displease him; she would still be tormented for an eternity. So Lisa did not care anymore. This was her reward for her denial of Jesus, the Son of the Only True God.

Satan just laughed at her response. Then he stared long and hard. Finally, in a low and calculated voice, he told her that her cousin Maria would be joining her in her new home. "That is my surprise for you!!!!"

"I will be placing her next to you. The two of you will be next door neighbors, together forever." Lisa jumped straight up and screamed at him, "You can't do that! She's only sixteen. You can't do that to her."

Satan turned to her, like the snake he is. He told Lisa, "I did not trick her. She chose me just as you did, because she wanted me. She wanted what I had to offer her. She was greedy and self-centered. The same as you were. Don't blame me for her choice. She knew exactly what she was getting. I only supplied what she asked for. That gave me the right to unleash my spirits on her. It was her choice. You know my enemy gave her the opportunity to choose Him. So give it a rest before I do something you will find very disheartening."

With that answer, Lisa crawled into her corner. Power and Prince of Night were ecstatic. They were laughing so hard. To the ordinary ear, it would have resembled loud growling. They were very pleased with how their master had handled Lisa.

Satan threw his cape over his shoulder and walked swiftly out of Lisa's quarters. He was on his way to the gate of Hell to personally meet Maria. He was going to enjoy this. She would be home in about 6 hours. He would wait for her and welcome her personally.

* * * * *

Karen has just walked into her home after returning from making funeral arrangements for Maria. She is tired and drained but she can't sleep. She stares at the spot on the floor where Maria had taken her last breath.

Suddenly the phone rings causing her to jump because of the loudness of the ringer in the silence of the home. It startled her to her core. When she answered, it was her friend Leali on the other end. She wanted to come over and keep her company, but Karen told her to come the next day instead. She needed to pray and get some answers. Karen told Leali, "I am going to get into and stay in Jesus' face until I find out what is going on in my family." Leali respected her need and told her, "I will talk with you tomorrow morning." They hung up and Karen began her conversation with Jesus.

Karen had been talking with her Savior, Jesus Christ, for about an hour when suddenly she stopped. She was impressed to listen and that is exactly what she did.

In His presence, for at least an hour, Karen kept silent. Suddenly she heard a loud sound that reminded her of a tornado. It came to mind that maybe she should head for the basement; but she couldn't move. Just as quickly as the sound began, it stopped. Slowly, Karen looked up because she felt an awesome presence in the room. What she saw caused great fear to fall upon her and she lowered her head. Immediately, she heard a soft, strong voice speak to her. "Karen, do not fear. I have come to give you answers and set you free from the generational curse on your family. Look at me." Karen looked up and saw Jesus smiling at her. He reached out His hand to her and she took it into her hand. Jesus led Karen to the sofa and the two of them sat down.

Jesus told Karen that she could handle the truth now and she would be free to do the work He had called her to do from the foundation of the world. He told her He was going to take her for a walk, back into her mother's womb. Karen looked at what appeared to be a familiar black circle. Jesus told her all these years she was looking at the inside of what had been her home from the time of conception until the day of her birth. She replied, "You mean, I have been looking at the inside of my mother's uterus all of this time. When I would become depressed and close my eyes or try to pray. This is what I could not get past? This has been like a curse." Jesus replied, "That is because it was an unwanted pregnancy in the beginning. Your mother did not think they could afford to have a child at the time. Finances were not the greatest and she thought your father would be upset. You picked up on the rejection immediately and that allowed the Spirit of Rejection to imprison you inside the womb."

"Follow Me and you will see what I mean." As they moved further back into the tunnel (the only way Karen could describe it to herself), it became very, very dark. Suddenly, they stopped in front of an old prison with a very big lock on the front door. The doorkeeper was huge, ugly and protective of his charge. He was ready to deal with Karen until he looked up and saw Jesus. Upon seeing Jesus, he fell on his face and trembled.

When Jesus stood in front of the door, the lock suddenly fell off by itself and the door opened.

Karen stood in front of the entrance. It was so dark and smelly inside that it made her gag. She could not see anything.

Jesus encouraged Karen to enter the dungeon. She moved slowly until, finally, she was inside. Somehow, it was familiar to her. There were a few happy moments, but mostly sad ones. She had not noticed that Jesus had entered the dungeon also. When she looked at Him, she saw something in His arms. He was holding it with such tender care and so very close to Him. As she looked close, she could see it was a baby. Jesus said, "Let's go." This time, Karen knew she was to follow and not move ahead of Him or in front of Him.

When they walked out of the dungeon, the door closed on its own. Jesus walked by the spirit guarding the door and never said a word. He didn't even glance in its direction. Karen stopped in front of the spirit. Anger rose up inside of her like she had never experienced before.

When Karen stopped walking, she was not aware that Jesus had stopped also. But He never looked around until she opened her mouth to curse the spirit.

Karen's voice was strong and full of power. "You foul Spirit of Rejection. You held me captive for all of these years but you no longer have a stronghold on my life. Jesus is my Lord, not you. I have His name to use against you and I do just that. You are loosed from your assignment against me. I have His Blood and I use that to cover myself completely. Now leave me and go back to your boss and wander in the dry places of this world."

At that command, the spirit let out a loud scream and disappeared. And with him, the dungeon also disappeared.

Jesus started walking again and Karen followed. She noticed that where it had been dark when they entered, now it was very light. She thought, "That spirit had caused the darkness in my mother's womb."

The baby in Jesus' arms caught Karen's attention. It was moving ever so slightly. Jesus was talking to the baby. Karen caught up to Jesus and was now walking side by side with Him.

She noticed they were now almost at the spot where they entered. Jesus stopped and looked at her. Then He laid the baby down on what appeared to be soft grass. Everything was so strange. She didn't know if she was dreaming or if this was an open vision. She could not tell. All she knew was that she felt as though something was happening on the inside of her.

When Karen looked at the baby closely, she realized it was her. But the color of the baby suggested it was dead. When Jesus put her down, she stopped moving. You could hardly hear the weak cry.

Karen moved closer to the baby. Then Karen began crying as though her heart would break. Jesus just stood there and monitored the whole scenario.

Finally, Karen sat on the soft grass next to the baby and picked her up. She held her, loved her and just talked to the baby. When Karen stopped crying and looked down at the baby; she saw the baby was healthy and beautiful. Jesus took the baby from Karen and again placed her on the soft grass.

The next scene was hard for Karen to believe. She watched herself growing up in front of own eyes. It was amazing. It was beautiful. She thought, "No one will ever believe this. But I know I am seeing it in order to help others like myself and even those who may be worse off than me."

When the baby had reached Karen's current age, she seemed to stop growing and aging. Jesus was standing there all the time. When the phenomenal act concluded, Jesus took her by the hand and led her to Karen. Karen's spirit joined its healthy self to her and she became strong in spirit, soul and body.

Karen knew immediately that she was not the same and would never be the same ever again. With that, she found herself back in the living room seated on the sofa with Jesus still sitting next to her.

He asked her if she was ready for the next phase. Karen replied that she was. So Jesus began telling her how kindred spirits draw similar spirits. He told her that is why people with the same problems marry into similar families.

"It is a kindred spirit – it draws strength from its own kind. Always remember that. As you minister to people, notice the spirit that has a stronghold on them.

The generational curse in your family is drugs and alcohol. It was introduced into your family by your forefathers. You know your family history. Check it over in your mind and all will be very plain to you. You've known it all the time but you did not realize it was a generational curse. That has been the stronghold in your family. Break it from over your life and it cannot stop you anymore.

You are whole and healthy now. Stay That Way. I am sending you out into the enemy's territory to pull in a lost generation from the fires of Hell.

You will be able to stand the fiery trials. I AM with you. Remember, I will not leave you. I am with you always. Stand fast and obey me. You know my voice. Do not move too quickly. When I tell you there is something wrong in any given situation, obey only Me. Do not lean to what man means to you. It will soon be worthless. Keep your heart set on winning souls."

After Jesus had ministered this to Karen, He released her hand and was gone.

* * * * *

eanwhile, Satan is awaiting Maria's arrival in Hell. He thinks to himself, "I am going to enjoy this. And when I am finished tormenting her; I will go visit her Aunt Karen. I think I will just kill her. It matters not to me if she goes to Heaven. At least, she will be out of my hair."

Something caught his attention. He gazes up and sees the final descent of Maria. When her feet touched down, he said, "Finally she is mine to rule."

When Maria comes through the gates with Greed, Intellect, Kingpin and Python; Satan stands up to greet her. This is something he only does on special occasions. "Welcome, Maria. Welcome Home! You have paid a great price to be here. Do you know what that price was?" Maria is trembling and crying. "Why cry now, Maria? You wanted this. You wanted me. You wanted my powers. Well, look around. All this belongs to you…you poor, stupid fool! My demons did a class act on you. But you wanted it so they let you have it."

"You didn't even last as long as Lisa. Oh, by the way, you and Lisa will be roomies. I decided to make you next door neighbors with her so get used to it! But, if that isn't good enough, do you remember how much better you thought you were than Lisa? Well, you are not any better. So Maria, I just want to welcome you home and let you know I've been waiting for you. Now follow me. Lisa is waiting for you too."

"Python and Intellect, follow me. Greed, go to the conference room and wait for me. Kingpin head back to earth and get with Pride and Lust. There is a new city I want to wage war against. They have your assignment with them." Kingpin heads for the earth once again as instructed.

Satan walked into Lisa's area. She knew he was there but she did not want to turn and face him because she knew her cousin was with him. Lisa could hear Maria sobbing softly.

Satan told Lisa to look at him. Reluctantly, she did. He had the biggest grin on his face. "I have company for you." Lisa told him "I don't need any company. Power and Prince of Night are enough company for me. Take her someplace else. You have plenty of spaces you can condemn her to."

Satan tells her, "Like it or not, she is

rooming with you. So get used to it. Maria, get in here!" Maria moves where Lisa can see her. Lisa snarled then grabbed Maria and started beating her. She called her foul, vulgar names. Lisa told her she was stupid, thinking she was so wise. "Maria, don't you know that there is 'No Second Chance' in Hell? Once you are here, that is it! IT IS FOR AN ETERNITY." She stopped beating her and went to her favorite spot. She spoke very softly, "Maria, No Second Chance. You lose Maria. You Lost." Entering the crowded area are Python and Intellect. Their job is to torment Maria for eternity.

Looking at the cousins and feeling very proud of himself, Satan decides to rub salt in the wounds. He mocks them saying, "Lisa and Maria, the two of you played my game and I won. Don't you realize that, on your own, you are not a match for me? You asked for certain things and I gave them to you. Whatever you lusted for, I granted. So now, you belong to me forever. And I will not even give Maria the same privilege of looking into Heaven as Lisa had.

Sometime later, Lisa, I will be visiting your mother and your aunt, Maria. I'm letting you know this because I will win her also.

You know as well as I how weak she is. She couldn't keep the two of you in line. Now that she has lost you both, I know I can beat her at every turn. Now I will leave the two of you for a while.

He made his way to the conference room. There, Greed was waiting for him to give his glorious report. Greed was very proud of himself. Satan congratulated Greed on a job well done. He told Greed to wait for him in the conference room. "Just relax and wait until I come back from my visit to the earth. I must visit with my great foe, Karen Kingslei. She must not get my children and give them to Jesus. I would hate to see that happen. I will see you when I return. Be thinking about your plan of action for your new assignment." When he finished instructing Greed, Satan left his throne room and headed for the earth.

* * * * *

Satan appeared in front of Karen's home. He looked around and noticed his stronghold was not as great as it had been in the past. This angered him a great deal. His messengers had not informed him about this change. He noted to himself, "I will deal with them upon my return to Hell." But, for now, he would give Karen a good going over for he felt she had something to do with it. If not her, he knew Jerry Green had a part in it.

Karen was getting ready to turn off the light on the night table when she felt the presence of something or someone in her room. Karen was seated on the edge of her bed and she looked towards the doorway. And there he stood. He was looking quite smug.

Satan finally spoke, "You will not leave this bedroom alive. I love your daughter and your niece. And you will be the next victim."

Karen gazed upon Satan. She did not have any fear, which to a degree surprised her. Then she realized that fear had been released from her when her spirit had been healed.

Karen spoke up, "You will not do anything to me. I am a Child of God." Satan was surprised by her answer and her boldness.

He had not seen that strength in her before. He tried to move towards her to pump fear into her heart.

Immediately, Karen spoke with more

boldness in her voice. "I have immunity in the Blood of Jesus – stay where you are. Do not come any closer or I will call forth the Warriors of Heaven against you."

Satan stopped in his tracks. By now, he is very confused. He recognized her boldness. He knew she had been with Jesus. But when did this take place? He figured it could not have been long. So, maybe, he could bluff his way through and beat her down.

He knew he could not move since she appropriated the Blood of His Enemy. But he did not want her to know this, so he tried to bluff his way in. He pretended he was going to move toward her.

Karen's voice was full of power and she repeated, "I Have Immunity in The Blood of Jesus and I Cover Myself Completely in the Blood Of Jesus. I use the powerful name of Jesus against you. You cannot Use Your Will To Do Any Harm To Me. I will tell you what I am going to do to your kingdom, Mr. Devil, since you invaded my private dwelling. You thought to kill me. Well, I am going to strip you of every soul that I can from out of your kingdom for my daughter that you took. I will take as many daughters from you that I can. For my niece that you stole, I will win all the nieces that I can. I am going to strip your kingdom. Instead of a stronghold in these cities, towns and countries you will become weak and Jesus will reign supreme. No longer will you kill babies or destroy young lives. I will set my face to the wall and cry out against you and then I will go out and take as many souls from you as I can. Once the young people and all people discover the terrible taskmaster that you are, they will run to Jesus. I am serving you notice as of this moment. You are the loser, I am the winner."

Satan looked at her. He is thinking to himself, "This is not the Karen Kingslei that I had been tormenting. This is someone else." He asked her, "Are You Karen Kingslei?" Karen never even answered him. She knew that Satan knew who she was. Karen was not going to play his game. She knew if he could get her into talking and using prideful words, she would lose her inner strength. It did not matter who she was but who Jesus is on the inside of her. He repeats, "Well, are you?" Karen never replied.

Satan was becoming very frustrated.

He came there to destroy her and she was upsetting his game plan.

Karen told Satan she was tired of his presence in her room and that this was to be his last visit to her. She told him that he was never to invade her privacy ever again and that the Holy Spirit is the only welcomed guest in her bedroom or the rest of her home. She told Satan that she'd had enough of his presence and that it was time for him to leave.

Satan knew that he had lost this one. But how could he give up? He thought to himself, "I should have come a day earlier. Then I know I would have had this person where she belongs, under my thumb. Satan didn't want to give up but he knew that his enemy must be close by. He kept looking around nervously, not knowing where his enemy would turn up. And if he did show up, he needed a way of escape. He thought, "I know I will defeat this Jesus but I have not come up with the plan yet. Oh, but I will! And when I do, Karen Kingslei will be one of my prizes."

Karen stood up and looked Satan directly in his eyes. She saw such evil and hatred. For her, this was a first. She had not seen the

Father of Evil face to face before and this was something that she did not ever want to forget.

With head held high, shoulders straight, eyes bright and piercing, in a voice clear and strong; Karen spoke, "Satan you will leave my home now in the Name of Jesus. You are not wanted here. NOW get out and be gone. You don't ever have any right to address me. I am not your child nor am I your slave. I belong to Jesus. You used to rule me in my life although I was saved and had accepted Jesus because I had not made Him Lord. I did not realize what I had in His Blood and His Name. Now I know what I have and who I am in Him. You caused my husband and my sister to die at a young age and go home. The only peace I have with that is knowing they are home with the Father."

"This one thing I do know and I will tell you by Almighty God; you will not take my life! You will not put sickness on me nor will you stop the work that I have been called to do. Souls will be pulled out of your kingdom. The souls we win will not be released until they are built up in their inner man so that they can bring down your kingdom."

"Finally, Satan let me remind you of this fact known by you and known by me. I do not have to listen to you. I have the authority in the name of Jesus to tell you to shut up and be silent. And you MUST obey. So do not open your mouth again, do not visit me again, and do not make yourself visible to me. I do not want to see you. You are not my master. Jesus is my master. Now, in the name of Jesus, whose I am and whom I serve, leave me! Leave my home! And those demons you left in my home to try and destroy me must also go-In The Name of Jesus. Now Go!!"

Satan did not have a choice. He knew something had gone dastardly wrong with his plan. He could not say a word. He looked up and there He stood, right behind Karen. His number one enemy was intensely staring at him with those eyes of fire and all around Him were Warrior Angels. He made a quick retreat and headed for Hell. He knew it was definitely conference time with his number one spirit, Greed.

* * * * *

ack in Hell's throne room, Satan and Greed are seated at the conference table. Greed inquired about his visit with Karen. Satan told Greed everything went just fine. Greed wanted to know why he had not killed her. Satan told Greed, "She isn't worth my time." He didn't want Greed to know that Karen had found out He couldn't kill her.

Satan finally started the meeting. He spoke up and said to Greed, "First things first. We must not allow the Church people to find out that the scripture John 10:10 does not apply to me. As long as they think I have the power to kill them, steal from them and destroy them and theirs; I have that kind of power over them. By their own mouths, they have given me that right. So keep them blind to this fact. Make sure they only read that verse, not above it or below it. Otherwise, they will find out that scripture means false pastors (shepherds), false prophets and teachers. You know the kind we have planted in the churches. If they find out, they will get rid of our teachers also. Keep them ignorant. Every time they quote that verse and give me the credit, it gives me the right to destroy them."

Greed nods in agreement to what his

master is speaking. Satan continues, "Greed, you must go back to earth and win more humans for me. We have lost a few. That is a few too many. I want them all; not one do I want to lose. Greed, always remembers this – one of our best weapons against these fools is their disbelief in me and the rest of you." Greed laughs at this. He said, "I know what you mean. We are just a figment of their imagination. We are just good old ghost stories." Then they both laughed. Satan tells Greed, "Another downfall of the human race is their lust. Of course, we can take credit for this also." They laugh again. "Poor, stupid fools. And they profess to be so intelligent."

Remember the lust of their flesh is very loud. The lust of their eyes is next in line. They see it then they want it. And, of course, there's Pride of Life. The eyes see it then the flesh wants it and must have it so pride of life can parade it around to the other humans. You, Pride and Lust will have to work together very closely. And do not forget about Kingpin. Work as one unit and get the job done.

Greed, remember that you are also the main downfall of the human race. You were birthed out of me. You are my exclusive creation. All humans, when born, are already fallen. Get them, if possible, before birth. Try to possess them from the womb. If that is not possible, try to get them at an early age.

Humans like the thrill and power that you give them. They enjoy the way you make them feel. They call it resourcefulness and ambition. They call it taking care of self. They even call it preparing for the future. Whatever it takes, win them over. Then the other spirits that have strong-holds over their family can gain more strength. Of course, there are those that we have lost to the enemy's camp. Do whatever you can to win them back. There is always a way."

He gives this assignment to Greed for Satan knows that the Chosen will not sell out even unto death. But he will not take the blame for it. He will blame Greed for failure. Even though he realizes it is not Greed's failure. He tells Greed that he is losing too many humans to the adversary, Jesus. "Greed, you are a master strategist. Get busy and win me more souls. We are getting too close to the next phase of war."

"Also keep the secret that, as long as humans walk in the natural realm, they will always have only natural desires. They will always want fleshly things in life. Keep them from going into the spirit

realm. *We must capture their thought life because then we can capture the whole person. But if they learn the secret of living by the Book that holds all the secrets of human success, we will run into problems. I know what makes them think they should only read the King James Version. Most humans can't understand the old Elizabethan English. Make them think the other versions are sinful. That should help our cause.*

Also, keep humans from communicating with Jesus by stopping them from praying or we will have a problem. They could win. If they insist on praying, get them into witchcraft or spiritualism. Have them become 'flakes'. Put them in touch with familiar spirits, anything but correct prayer. So remember, do not let them read the Book. Allow them to read anything but the Book. Also, do not allow them to pray. They can do anything but pray according to the Book. If they put the two of them together correctly, they can do a lot of harm to us. I hate to think about how much damage they could do. Do you understand?

So far, we have a whole lost generation practically to ourselves. Go out and bring the fruit of this lost people to me. Do you think you can handle this assignment?"

Greed knows that it is a very challenging assignment but he likes what it offers…more souls for his master's kingdom and more assurance for him to keep the first chair. He must always remain number one. He was in the Garden and he was also in Heaven with his master. He will not become second for anyone or anything.

He told Satan that he welcomes the challenge. "To win humans is easy. Give them what they want and they skip away happy. Sometimes, withhold it for a while and make them desire it more. I really can't see a problem. All humans have me or will have me in them."

"You saw that in the Garden. Remember? Don't worry. I can do the job."

"When do you want me to start the newest adventure?" Satan answered, "As soon as this conference is over, you are to head for earth immediately. There are three people in the city of Halal that I want you to be aware of…Jerry and Leali Green along with Karen Kingslei. They are big trouble. Don't let your guard down for a minute where these three are concerned. They spell trouble. Put spies on them and keep spies on them. Make sure they keep notes. Have them report to you on a regular basis then you report back to me, especially when there is an emergency. Karen said something about doing damage to our kingdom but she did not say exactly what her plans are. She is a real troublemaker."

"Are there any questions?" Greed shakes his head no then Satan dismisses him. "This meeting is over. Head for the earth and catch up with Pride, Lust and Kingpin." Greed stands and pays homage to his king. Then he heads back to the earth. His intent is to conquer this generation of Lost Souls.

* * * * *

Meanwhile, Karen is leaving out of her front door and heading out to wherever the Holy Spirit leads her to win the same generation of souls. He is sending her to the same location where Greed is headed......